Summary

Not all marketing knowledge is equal. Deep marketing smarts are learned informally, over time, and through firsthand life experiences. As a start-up entrepreneur, you have a gap between what you know and what you need to know.

Beyond Start-Up Lane is a marketing crash course e-book framed to trigger your thinking and deepen your marketing smarts. Here are 100 marketing questions for you to answer. Check your beliefs and opinions against mine. Validate your marketing expertise. Decide what smarts you need to learn and assemble in-house...and which do you need to beg, borrow, or buy to grow.

In the end, you'll achieve deeper marketing smarts which will help you find and keep clients.

Author's Note to the Reader

One of the dead Greek philosophers said that nothing exists except atoms and empty space – everything else is opinion.

So, in my opinion...

...A **start-up** is an idea looking to stand on its own in the market place – which means it has value to somebody at a profit.

...**Start-up entrepreneurs** are the people on fire for the idea – they either prove their idea to be self-sufficient or bury it in the Graveyard of Good Intentions.

...**Start-Up Lane** is the mythical pathway found in the minds of start-up entrepreneurs – where their idea begins to be proved.

What happens on Start-Up Lane mirrors start-up reality. Entrepreneurs who find the guts to jump the gate find the Lane to be dark, crooked, rough, uphill, and confining. The entrepreneurs bring the only sunshine to Start-Up Lane ...

Start-Up Lane consists of two elements – one mental and one physical.

It is the mental ground where entrepreneurs…

…identify what they know against what they don't know.

…explore how their idea can be provided for, protected, processed, promoted, prototyped, piloted, and then personally sold to new clients.

Start-Up Lane is also the physical ground where…

…what has been learned is converted to real world experiments to determine if their idea lives or dies. Legal. Patent. Organize. Test. Adapt. Test. Adapt.

Fail to scale.

Start-up entrepreneurs remain in the Lane until their idea is underground or under blue sky. Unfortunately, many start-up entrepreneurs who become viable and begin seeing ~~their blue~~ fail to scale.

They discover quickly that post-viability marketing of their idea is totally different than pre-viability marketing. Their charm, integrity, looks, and forcefulness walked them through Start-Up Lane, but couldn't get them up to speed beyond it.

You're on Start-Up Lane…right?

It's no picnic ground. You are totally focused on the Start-Up Lane exploration and experimental phases. I get it. My guess is that you are devoting little thinking and energy to what happens when you can go beyond the Lane.

But, consider this…

…when you do get beyond Start-Up Lane…savvy marketers will not concede any marketspace to you. You will find crowded and competitive markets crammed with street fighting marketers who eat newbies like you for snacks.

These sharks have deep marketing smarts and will not give an inch because you have a new mousetrap. They could care less about the promises you need to keep, benefactors you need to benefit, or the virgin vision you need to pursue – unless of course you hire them…

So, in my opinion...

You have a marketing knowledge gap right now. Regardless of its size, what you know and who you know will not get you where you want to go beyond the Lane.

Marketing is not a department. It is all the activities associated with driving demand and optimizing profits. Learning the art and science behind this takes a good chunk of marketing smarts.

You'll need deeper marketing smarts post Lane to avoid slipshod decisions and stone-cold brokenness. Speed learning late will put you at risk. You need to start now while in the Lane. Plus, it makes sense to learn some of the basic marketing rules now so you can break them later.

100 thought-provoking Marketing ABCs.

Beyond Start-Up Lane is a marketing crash course e-book created to help you cultivate deeper marketing smarts and close your knowledge gap. This e-book asks 100 marketing questions to trigger your marketing thinking.

Your answers can test your beliefs and opinions against mine...validate your current marketing smarts...and possibly identify what smarts you need to learn, assemble in-house, or buy.

Each question is individually wrapped in a short story to provide some context for your answer. Some are written real-dead serious. Some more whimsical. Some past generational. Some are in order. Most are not. Some concepts are revisited in other ABCs. Some questions you will skip. Some you will wonder how it's marketing related.

Hopefully, you'll start to understand that marketing is not about finding clever ways to sell you idea, but help your clients be better off. Oops. Spoiler alert!

So, in my opinion...

Beyond Start-Up Lane is how you informally start learning about marketing while you are gaining firsthand life experience with your idea. The more answers you understand and the faster you understand them will be directly proportional to the deepening of your marketing smarts...which increases your ability to find and keep clients.

Keep moving to your rising sun. Let's get going...

Willie

Willie has chunks of deep smarts. He uniquely mixes 22 years of criminal justice experience with 28 years of marketing practice. He is recognized as a marketing expert who simplifies the complex world of marketing for independent businesses. He is most noted as being a marketing strategist, and has taught numerous seminars on that topic.

He specializes in education-based marketing, and is a skilled copywriter who has written and developed successful, radio, TV, direct mail, and print advertising campaigns. He has previously authored two books. He is currently on Start-Up Lane himself as a managing member in Right Time, a faith-based start-up company committed to the prosocial reintegration of criminal offenders. He may be contacted at williedavis@beyondstartuplane.com

Acknowledgements

To give credit to all those who have contributed to these writings would take a separate volume. No book of this nature is really written by one author. Deep smarts come from endless hours of reading marketing books written by very smart people. Deep smarts are acquired through life experiences and much is owed to the hundreds of paying clients who have given me the opportunity to serve them while learning from them. Deep smarts comes from attending and giving tons of marketing seminars over the past 20 years. I would give special recognition to the Wizard Academy in Austin, TX, by far the deepest and craziest learning I have ever done. And finally, a pay forward thank you to all the start-up entrepreneurs who turn these small thoughts into real-world actions.

Contents

#91 HAVE YOU NOTICED THAT YOUR CLIENTS SPEND A LOT OF PRETTY PENNIES?

#92 WHY IS THE WORD DISCRIMINATION PROFITABLE?

#93 WILL YOUR PEOPLE HAVE ORDINARY JOBS?

#94 WHO IS IN CHARGE OF YOUR ORGANIZATION?

#95 CAN YOU MAKE THINGS HUM IN YOUR MILL?

#96 IS MUTUAL ADJUSTMENT THE SILVER BULLET YOU"RE LOOKING FOR TO STRENGTHEN YOUR ORGANIZATION?

#97 CAN YOU THINK SERVE INSTEAD OF SELL?

#98 CAN YOU IMPROVE YOUR MANAGEMENT THROUGH BETTER THINKING?

#99 IS "RIDING HERD" A LEGITIMATE MANAGEMENT STYLE?

#100 WHATJA THINK?

22 Idiotic Quotes...

...here you'll find 22 quotes to lift your start-up spirits. These are idiotic quotes made by 'deep smarts' people who thought they could see in the future. After reading them, you should flush any thought you are chasing a wild Start-Up Lane idea that should be buried in the graveyard.

This is the first of your 100 marketing ABCs.

99 left.

If you think about this first question first…the remaining 99 ABCs will help harmonize your marketing symphony. Failure to address this question and the 99 will quaver like a Junior High School band.

It's a deceptively simple question…

WHAT IS YOUR PURPOSE?

Purpose is a simple statement of intent…why are you, a start-up entrepreneur, doing what you are doing?

Are you discovering something? Are you making something better? Improving people's lives? Defending or advocating a cause? How about following a religious/spiritual calling? Are you doing what you are doing to make a profit? Or something else?

Why is it important to define and focus on your purpose?

Your purpose will get you up in the morning. It will give you pride. It will motivate you to do better. It will give your life meaning. It might give you a competitive advantage in the marketplace.

Your purpose will shape your strategy and influence your decisions. Your purpose, when defined and refined, will energize everything about your organization, including your marketing.

It's not important that you perfect your statement of purpose now. Eloquence of verbiage can be improved later.

What is important is that you start thinking about it. Because, when it's time to roll, breakout, or scale, your purpose will need to have been fully formed in order to gain significant market ground.

Will you be a symphony…or a junior high school band?

First ABC of three on Purpose…next…

IS PROFIT YOUR CHOICE OF PURPOSE?

Not a good choice. Sorry.

There are some smart people who argue well that profit maximization *is* the purpose of a company. Company directors have a fiduciary duty to its shareholders. Maximizing profits is the believed path to creating happiness in life. More reasons...

There are also some smart people who argue well that profit is not a purpose. Instead, it's an *objective*. Profit is necessary and yes, it's gratifying. But, it's not a purpose. I'm with this group. I believe that profit is validation of your purpose.

Here's some sorting out help for you:

Think profit maximization is your purpose and test it against these questions:

Will others want to follow it? Will it give them energy and motivate them to get up in the morning? Could it give you a competitive advantage? Could it be the driving force that shapes your strategy and guides managerial decisions?

Now, select a purpose that has a high measure of moral integrity like, say, curing cancer. Test it against the same questions.

Surprisingly, the answers to both sets are...yes!

However, here's the truth. People will flock to the one with a moral cause. We humans want meaning and significance in our lives and consequently we are drawn to those who help us with our self-actualization. Profit maximization as your purpose will leave you like a barking dog on the porch of your chosen markets...wanting to get in.

Some entrepreneurs begin Start-Up Lane with a clearly identified purpose. Some develop it along the way, while others never develop one at all. Once in the market, some companies tell you unabashedly and up front that they are all about money, money, money. Some will not walk the moral purpose they talk, while others wear their purpose on their sleeve as a badge of honor.

At some point you will decide if, how, and how much you are going to package your purpose to the world. But first, you must look inside yourself and clearly identify why you are really doing what you are doing.

Second ABC of three on Purpose...next...

"One must be something, in order to do something."

- Johann Wolfgang von Goeth

You will soon begin to conceptualize the organization that wraps around your idea. How that gets accomplished has changed.

We have moved on from an Industrial Age command-and-control organizational structure that rigidly placed machines and people in their predictable places, like cogs and wheels. Unfortunately, today many organizations still operate this way.

What is replacing this methodology is a different style of organizational structure based on the concept of self-interest being inseparable from community interest...where the good of the individual and the good of the whole are the same. This idea is really not new – it is illustrated well in Adam Smith's *Wealth of Nations.*

Successful organizations of the future start with a shared and common purpose that is embraced by those who believe in it. The purpose binds the group.

After purpose come principles. Principles are the living moral guidelines within your organization. You might set the direction, but your people will finalize through their actions how the whole and parts will conduct themselves in pursuit of the purpose.

After purpose and principles are established, the next important ingredient is people. People who believe in your purpose and practice and principles will join you. Those who truly support your purpose and practice the principles will be the right people who will guide your organization to success.

Only after purpose, principles, and people do you start working on structure and processes. I know. This is pretty deep stuff to hit you with while you are in the process of proving you have an idea that will be of value to someone. Enough said.

ARE YOU AN ORGANIZATION OF THE FUTURE?

If so, it starts with purpose, followed by principles, people, structure, and finally, processes. This is worth some additional thought.

Three ABC of three on Purpose...done...

Organizational culture is the way people think and act. Your organization will have a culture. Actually, you will have two cultures – formal and informal.

Think of it as an iceberg.

Your formal culture is above the water…the total collection of your purpose, principles, structure, policies, and processes. It's what is written in your employee manual and on your bulletin board.

The informal culture is below the water…your employees' reaction to your formal culture. It's how they act behind your back. It's how things really get done behind the scenes.

You will have a problem when your informal culture overshadows your formal culture. If you have the wrong employees, they will push back on your initiatives.

You try to manage the non-productive climate with extended training, or worse, top-down mandates enforced by rewards and punishments. They continue to push. The cycle continues and productivity is jeopardized.

Savvy leaders are discovering that trying to manage or change cultures through antiquated, hierarchical, command-and-control methods of the past are counterproductive. Employees won't walk what the management talks, no matter how often that talk is reviewed, trained, or reinforced.

The answer is to build the organizational cultures right in the first place.

Hang on. Here we go again…

You start with purpose, then principles, and then people. The right people in the right place in concert with purpose and principles will turn your cultural iceberg upside down.

CAN YOU SEE YOURSELF AS A CULTURE ARCHITECT BASED ON YOUR PEOPLE?

The world thrives on innovation.

Unfortunately, many entrepreneurs will at some point in their start-up life, buy into either the Mousetrap or Field of Dreams myth.

Ralph Waldo Emerson is credited with saying, "If a man can make a better mousetrap than his neighbor...the world will make a beaten path to his door."

The truth is that many mousetraps have been invented since the original. However, we still use the original because it works cheaply and we can throw it away with the dead. Just saying...

James Earl Jones' character, Terrance Mann, in the 1989 classic movie *Field of Dreams* tells Kevin Costner's character, Ray Kinsella, that people will come to the idiotic baseball field out in the land of nowhere. "Ray, people will come."

Well, at the end of the movie, people did come. And, they came in real life too. For the next 20 years the real-life Iowa baseball field drew about 65,000 tourists annually. The farm containing the "Field" sold in 2011 for a price believed to be around $5.4 million. Just saying...

But here's the truth. New mousetraps and baseball fields in the middle of corn fields don't just magically draw people because they exist. You are a little out of touch with reality if you believe that your idea will take on a magnetic life of its own just because it came from your brain and occupies space.

People need to be persuaded. Period. That persuasion is what marketing is all about.

Inventors of new mousetraps have done a poor job of persuading.

And who would visit that cornfield with the hopes of possibly seeing the ghost of their father without first having seen the movie? You can bet this movie has been seen by millions of guys wishing one more moment with Dad.

YOU'RE NOT GOING TO BUY INTO THE MOUSETRAP MYTH, ARE YOU?

Start thinking how you are going to persuade the world to see your baseball field.

An innovation is an idea, practice, or object that is perceived to be new.

Yes, there are inventions that are a decade old, but that are new to me now. To me...it is an innovation.

Your innovation is as new as it is perceived by people. There are probably Aboriginal Australian tribes for whom electricity would be perceived as an innovation.

The more important question is...

HOW DISRUPTIVE IS YOUR INNOVATION?

A disruptive innovation is a concept identified in the mid-1990s by Clayton Christensen. Innovations surface at the bottom of a market and eventually displace established businesses.

Big box discount retailers displaced full service department stores. Community colleges displaced four-year universities. Medical clinics displaced traditional doctor's offices. And you certainly know what the cell phone has done to the landline phone...

The degree of disruption your innovation creates will be directly proportional to the difficulty you have in bringing it to market.

This is a hard concept for start-up entrepreneurs to grasp.

I mention it now because when people tell you that you have disruptive technology or a disruptive innovation, you can smile...but know that you have a tremendous task ahead of you as you scale it to market.

Don't give up. It can be done.

Accept this as gospel - getting your innovation adopted and embedded in the marketplace will be difficult...even after you have proven it viable...even when it has obvious advantages.

There are five stages your potential client will experience as your product or service innovation becomes embedded in their organization.

First, they must learn about what you have. You have to offer them knowledge that is more interesting than what they currently have. It's about enlightening them. (1)

Next, they must begin forming a favorable impression about you. You want them to deliberate on your innovation. We don't do anything until we first visit it in our mind. (2)

Then, you then want for their resistance to be lowered so they say 'Yes! I will buy'. Short tap dance here. (3)

After your happy dance, you must help them implement your product or service into their processes. You can't just let them buy and walk away. (4)

Lastly, you need to hang around long enough to see that there is confirmation. You want them to know they made the right decision. (5)

ARE YOU GOING TO SELL OR EMBED YOUR INNOVATION?

Have you thought about the process? Have you thought about the sales cycle?

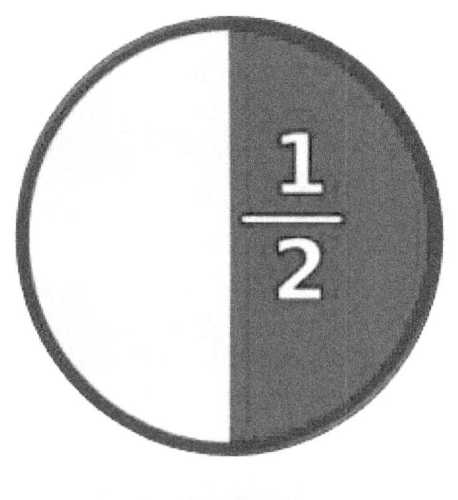

Fractions. Ugh!

I always thought reducing fractions to their lowest common denominator was a useless academic exercise until I became associated with marketing.

In our KEEP IT SIMPLE STUPID (KISS) world, the concept of reducing everything to its lowest common denominator is almost mandatory.

½ OFF is better than 2/4 OFF – because it's simpler.

This is especially true for the word MARKETING!

A gazillion words have been written on the subject of marketing and its definition can be extremely confusing...unless you reduce it to its lowest common denominator.

One definition of marketing...all the activities associated with finding and keeping profitable customers (10 words)...

CAN YOU REDUCE HOW MARKETING GETS DONE TO SIX WORDS?

Well, I did and now I'm going to give them to you. Ready?

What you say. What you do.

The truth is that everything you do to influence potential clients to see it your way can be reduced and categorized into these six words.

Marketing is not confusing. When reduced to its simplest terms it provides a logical guideline to make all kinds of decisions.

Want to convince your math teacher that you are a whiz at fractions? Don't just tell him. Show him.

Want your potential client to show interest? Tell him about all the reasons he should.

Then, do what you said!

It's just simple math.

Start-up Lane marketing relies mostly on sweat equity and personal sales. It's about discovering that you have something that solves someone else's problem and that they are willing to pay for it. Pre-viability marketing is just getting you into the game. Toe in the water thing.

Scale-up marketing relies on sweat equity, personal sales, and 'everything else.' It's about rolling out to the world what your start-up marketing proved. It's this 'everything else' in scale-up marketing that confuses most entrepreneurs. And rightfully so.

'Everything else' opens up a huge marketing vocabulary: marketing plan, marketing mix, marketing communications, markets, demographics, advertising, public relations, direct mail, direct response, targets, copywriting, website, lead generation, strategy, tactics, branding, your mother, second cousin, Dr. Seuss, etc...

How do you unscramble this dictionary mess? Don't pay any attention...at least not yet. .

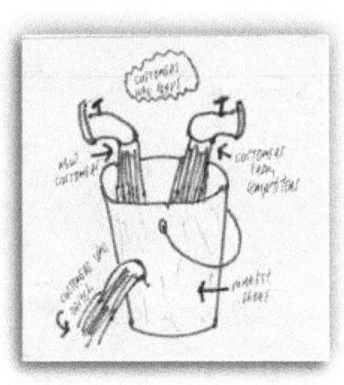

Think Marketing Napkinology! The ability to sit in a booth at McDonald's and sketch a marketing concept on a napkin so that the other person in your booth understands it.

ARE YOU READY FOR SOME NAPKINOLOGY?

Here are 7 quick-hit marketing concepts that I believe start-up entrepreneurs should be able to napkin over a Big Mac with a stranger. These 7 are the next 17 ABCs...buckle up!

The Marketing/Sales Iceberg (1 ABC)

Value Mathematical Formula (4 ABCs)

The 3-7-90 Rule (3 ABCs)

How Retail Traffic is Increased (3 ABCs)

The Four Personalities (2 ABCs)

I of the Storm (3 ABCs)

Leaky Bucket (1 ABC)

Get these 7 down and then you can start with the rest of the vocabulary.

Marketing has faced an identity crisis for some time now.

Another iceberg?

While the word *sell* can be traced back to biblical times, the term *marketing* didn't appear until after the Industrial Revolution.

Marketing was seen as less tacky and a little classier of a word than sales...a little polish goes a long way.

Actually, marketing and sales are two very different functions with little in common.

Marketing is more comprehensive that selling. It is defined as all the activities that are involved in creating and keeping devoted followers. Marketing is the entire iceberg.

Sales are a function of marketing, a single activity that influences a potential client to purchase your specific product or service. Sales would only be the tip of the iceberg

Both marketing and sales are noble professions to for who understand them.

Unfortunately, shady salespeople and deceitful selling practices have established a tremendous frustration and mistrust from the public regarding those who produce what the public needs.

Therefore, the modern marketplace holds sales in low esteem, and by association, marketing gets the same black eye. The belief is that it's all about shaking loose change from your pocket.

Marketing's identify crisis should not be your identify crisis. Be proud that you are a marketer. No guilt with any part of the marketing iceberg. But, to succeed beyond Start-Up Lane, you must instinctively separate marketing and sales. And, more importantly, get rid of any guilty you may have on the sales profession.

YOU DON'T HAVE SALES GUILT DO YOU?

This is Marketing/Sales Napkinology one of one...done...

You should always understand that *money moves* and it's perfectly acceptable for it to move from a potential client to you.

This is the nature of things.

This sounds rather callous, especially after strongly stating that I believe profit is not a purpose. Profit is one of your chief marketing aims.

You must get money to move from your clients to you and you need to know how it is done.

You can start with this visual...

If you visited the worst neighborhood in your hometown and selected twenty families at random and proceeded to give each family $1,000 each week for the next five weeks, and then revisited them again in ten weeks to find out what they did with the money, you'll discover that the money is not in a bank account or under a mattress. It has moved somewhere.

Best Buy? Verizon? Somewhere?

Their money is not finite. It's replenishable.

Same with your potential client. They get more all the time.

Money moves from people who would prefer to exchange it for something else, to those who happily, expectantly, and guiltlessly welcome it.

Mother Teresa believed this. People were happy to give and she was happy to receive. No guilt. Nada. None.

CAN YOU SMILE LIKE MOTHER TERESA?

She definitely understood the 'Dance of the Dollar.'

This is Value Mathematical Formula Napkinology one of four...next ABC...

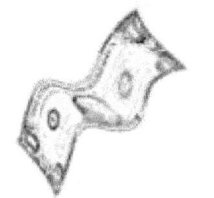 Now, before you have a cow and think I'm a heartless bastard when I tell you that money moves and you should smile like a guiltless Mother Teresa...understand that this is the 'Dance of the Dollar' in a free-market society.

One of the prerequisites for your successful marketing is being 100% psychologically and emotionally OK with this 'Dance'. Here's how it works.

The 'Dance of the Dollar' is money moving in exchange for value. This is the key.

You cannot print money. It's illegal. You cannot steal money. It's against the law. However, there is nothing stopping you from creating as much value as possible. That's right. Value.

(Time out here. We're going deeper in the next ABC to understand the concept of value. We're even going to do it mathematically so that you easily understand how it's scored. But, before that...you have got to get comfortable with the 'Dance.' Hopefully, this will help you.)

Everyone's dancing.

AREN'T NON-PROFIT RELIGIOUS GROUPS AND CHARITIES DANCING FOR THEIR DOLLARS?

They are creating value and you are donating. The dollar is dancing because money is moving from you to them...and it moves because of the value they create for you. Sadly, these secretive sellers may be the same people that look down their noses at the unscrupulous used car salesman...but the dance is the same. It's just hidden behind different intentions and reasons.

The 'Dance' is also happening with Susie down the street at the local strip club. Single mom. Two kids. Guy dollars are exchanged for her value nightly that puts food on her kids' table.

Don't get hung up on judging the value here. Just understand that money is going to move and value is the reason dollars dance for it.

Now, it's time to understand this concept of value.

This is Value Mathematical Formula Napkinology two of four...next ABC...

The word value is used so much in today's marketing that it means nothing. It's a great value. I value your friendship. It rolls off our back like shower water. Yuk!

However, since value is the key to getting dollars to dance their way to your bank account...you must understand what it is. Once you understand and begin applying it, your marketing world will erupt like a volcano.

Promise.

Value is defined as: V=PE-P. Value equals Personal Experience minus Price.

Personal experience is subjective. Price is set.

If you think that the personal experience you gained in your last buying decision was greater than the price you paid...then you (in your perception) received value. Money moved from you to the seller. Seller is happy. You are happy (maybe).

Think of the mathematical formula vertically.

Your job as a start-up entrepreneur is to create as much space vertically between your potential client's personal experience and your asking price.

The greater the difference between their PE and your P...the greater the value.

Your job as a start-up entrepreneur is to establish a profitable price and create a personal experience above that price.

When the personal experience is greater than the asking price...dollars dance from one hand to another. PE>P=S

Want to make a lot of money? (It's moving all around you). Create a lot of space between your client's personal experiences and the price of your product.

WAS VALUE CREATED IN YOUR LAST PURCHASE?

This is Value Mathematical Formula Napkinology three of four...next ABC...

All together now….

…marketing is a noble profession. I don't have any hidden, subconscious guilt about being a marketer.

I am not a seller is attempting to unscrupulously seduce buyers into spending more than originally intended, buying pricier options, or simply buying when no purchase was intended.

I understand that money moves. It's swirling all around me. Attracting it is a validation of my purpose, not the reason for it.

How I attract the money that is moving is to create value. Because money moves in exchange for value. There is no limitation, probation, or restriction on how much value I can create.

I understand the two critical mathematical formulas:

V=PE-P   PE>P=S

Value is the space created between the Personal Experience and Price. When the Personal Experience I create is greater than the Price I'm asking…the dollars dance to me. The greater the space…the more dancers show up on my stage. .

Warning. The space between the PE and P can be created two ways…raising the Personal Experience or lowering the Price.

A sale is nothing more than an attempt to create value by the latter. Retailers are infamous for having constant discount offers in hopes that potential customers will darken their doors for the perceived value.

The better route is to raise the Personal Experience, not lower the price. Remember, it's all about the space between the PE and P.

CAN YOU NOW DIAGRAM HOW YOU CREATE WEALTH?

This is Value Mathematical Formula Napkinology four of four…done…

If your new business is retail...if you have a brick-and-mortar establishment where people come to you to buy...these next three crash courses are for you.

If your new business is not retail...understanding these next crash courses will still benefit you. Don't just pass on them. They are good brain food.

Your retail traffic is created by the relationship between your Share of Voice (SOV) and Impact Quotient (IQ).

SOV is your percentage of advertising compared to your competition. This is determined by your media representative's ability to deliver on your allotted budget.

There is always one business in a market that has an abundance of money for advertising because you cannot escape their voice wherever you turn. It's generally a car dealership. TV. Radio. Print. Flyers. The quality of the ad makes no difference. It's all about quantity.

IQ is the measure of power of influence of your advertising. Your message's relevance is the responsibility of your copy writer. If it is meaningful enough it may need to be said only once to get a response. Powerful IQs move the world.

WANT TO INCREASE YOUR RETAIL TRAFFIC?

A convincing message with a small budget will whip a bulky budget with an unconvincing message every time. Work on developing a better and more powerful message.

This is Retail Traffic Napkinology one of three...next ABC...

Your retail sales are generated by your clients' Personal Experience (PE) with your business. PE is entirely your responsibility. Not your media rep's. Not your copy writer. You.

Your advertising will not make you better at what you do. It will only accelerate what was going to happen anyway. Positive word-of-mouth advertising is all about the personal experience.

ARE YOU DELIVERING WHAT YOU PROMISED?

This is Retail Traffic Napkinology two of three...next ABC...

Do the retail math. Plug in any set of numbers to see how the relationship between SOV, IQ, and PE has on your retail sales.

WHICH RETAILER (LEFT OR RIGHT) HAS THE GREATEST SALES WITH THE FEWEST ADVERTISING DOLLARS?

It won't take a long look to see how the Personal Experience can save you tons of money!

Note: These numbers are fictitious. They are there to demonstrate the relationships.

$$7 \leftarrow \textbf{SOV} \rightarrow 2 \rightarrow 1$$

$$^{\times}2 \leftarrow \textbf{× IQ} \rightarrow 5 \rightarrow 7$$

$$\overline{14} \leftarrow \textbf{T} \rightarrow 10 \rightarrow 7$$

$$^{\times}1 \leftarrow \textbf{× PE} \rightarrow 4 \rightarrow {}^{\times}8$$

$$\overline{14} \leftarrow \textbf{S} \quad \overline{40} \rightarrow 56$$

This is Retail Traffic Napkinology three of three…done…

3 %

Here's your innovation problem. The world is not paying attention.

Pick any industry. Pick any market. Here are the percentages you can use as a foundation to help in your marketing efforts.

- 3% of the market is ready to buy.

- 7% of the market has thought about it.

- 90% of the market is not thinking about it.

This week, in the city where you live…3% of people are shopping for furniture, shoes, chain saws, security fencing, etc.,…7% have thought about buying something…and 90%, well, they flat out know they aren't interested even if what you have is free. Think free kittens.

Of course, these percentages are not exact. They fluctuate up and down but are important because they help divide the market. A larger percentage of children's shoes will be bought the week of Easter and right before school starts as opposed to Super Bowl week. Furniture sales spike during three day weekends as both husband and wife are together.

Businesses advertise when the percentages are up and don't when the percentages are down. Weight loss in January. Tax preparation in February. Toys in November. Wine sales in December.

Two things to take away from this.

First, the majority of sellers target their messages to the 3% and the 7%. Very few target their communications to the 90%. Note: Smart marketers and those with resources target the 90% because they know the 90% will eventually become the 7% and 3% and they want to be the first thought about when that time comes.

Second, if you have a disruptive innovation unknown to the marketplace…you might not even have the 3%. Talk about a tough row to hoe…

WHAT PERCENTAGE ARE YOU TARGETING?

This is 3-7-90 Rule Napkinology one of three…next ABC…

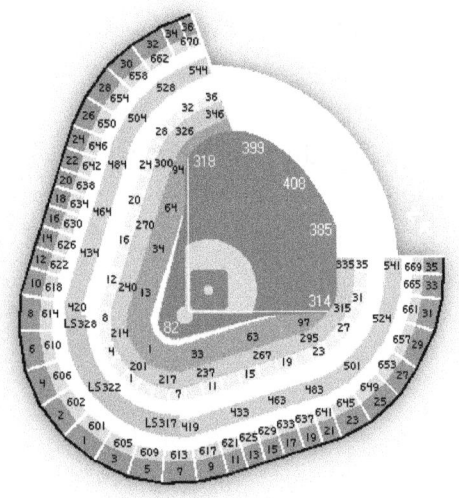

Education-based marketing is an information seeking and information processing strategy in which an individual reduces uncertainty about the advantages and disadvantages of your product or service.

Chet Holmes had a great example of Education-based marketing – The Stadium Pitch.

Imagine you are in a giant stadium where the entire audience is composed of your most perfect potential clients.

You have the opportunity to present to them all at once. Your potential clients had to come, but they didn't have to stay. If what you say to them is of no interest, they can simply get up and leave.

If you start pitching your product's features people will get trampled as they leave quickly. If you start talking about how your products might benefit their business, some will stay as they may be in the market to buy now. But, sadly most will leave.

How you get them glued to their seats is to teach them something of *value*. Later you can weave in how your product or service helps them. I'm not talking about a veiled sales pitch here. Really teach them something. You're the expert.

SO, WHAT COULD YOU SAY IN THE STADIUM THAT WOULD KEEP EVERYONE IN THEIR SEATS?

This is 3-7-90 Rule Napkinology two of three…next ABC…

WHO TAUGHT YOU TO TIE YOUR SHOES?

My Grandfather taught me and I never had to be taught again. Learned once.

Never forgot.

Same with the bicycle.

So, why wouldn't that also apply to your marketing? Shouldn't you create a marketing curriculum that teaches as it sells?

A *curriculum* is a learning system that teaches one bit of information at a time. Each marketing message (bit) can build on the learning of the previous one.

It can teach your target why your business is superior and why he should patronize you.

You are not going to stop offering him reasons to raise his hand at some point. Keep track of all your marketing messages directed at your target.

With all of them assembled together, do they constitute a curriculum?

This is 3-7-90 Rule Napkinology three of three…done…

It goes all the way back to ancient Greeks. They figured it out.

There are only four basic personalities in this world. Myers-Briggs breaks them down into 16 categories with four letter names. Others classify personalities by color, animals, etc. Whether I'm yellow, purple, a dolphin or an elephant...there are only four basic personalities.

Personality #1 is the bottom line guy. Give me the facts. Don't mess with me about stories. Personality #2 understands #1 but goes further by wanting proof. OK, I see your bottom line. I want to know how that works. Give me the details. Personality #3 is all about the relationships. Kumbaya. Family. Love you brother. Personality #4 is in the moment. Don't know what happened five minutes ago and don't care what happens five minutes from now. It's all about now.

The world is fairly evenly comprised of these four basic personality types – about 25% each. Each of us has some of all four personalities inside us. However, we all differ in the order and strength of each component.

Smart TV people understand the four personalities. Ensemble TV casts are built around the four personalities. Star Trek (Kirk, Spock, Bones, Scottie). Sex and the City. Friends. All four personalities are represented in these series because writers know that we'll watch our TV personality soul-mate. Represent all four and you have four times the audience .

You may not know these personalities by clinical terms, but you do know them sub-consciously. Walk into a seminar mixer and you'll gravitate to your dominant personality type. Become a retail shopper and see how many sales people you have to inform that you are just looking.

A lot of people these days think race is our main bias. Actually, personality is the first bias.

ARE YOU AWARE THAT PERSONALITIES AFFECT YOUR BUSINESS?

This is Four Personalities Napkinology one of two...next ABC...

The more you learn about the four basic personalities the better your sales presentations will be. The more you understand the four basic personalities the more persuasive your website will be.

Personality #1: Wants to cut to the chase – now!

 Personality #2: Understands the chase. Wants proof.

Personality #3: Wants to know where the human connection comes in.

Personality #4: Party time!

All four personalities will be sitting in your seminar room. You can guess, but won't know for sure, which personality is in front of your sales or investment pitch. And, all four personalities will be visiting your website.

HOW DO START-UP ENTREPRENEURS PITCH TO THE FOUR PERSONALITIES?

Your safe bet is to open up your talk to Personality #1. Cover in the first 30 seconds or 90 words what will be included in the rest of the time. Like a 'table of contents'.

Next, offer Personality #2 the proof they need.

At the end of your talk or copy, make sure you let the Personality #3 people know that you care about them.

And what about Personality #4? While you are talking, do a magic act. And for the website? Include visually appealing materials (pictures and colors) throughout. They don't read much.

This is Four Personalities Napkinology two of two…done…

As you exit Start-Up Lane and enter your business life, you will eventually find yourself in the 'I of the storm'. As the business owner you will be pressured from all sides.

*...**pressing down on you*** are your higher authorities. These are people, such as your family, of whom you have a personal desire to take care of while you run your company. Your decisions always have their best interests at heart. Plus, your shareholders, outside government agencies – all, from time to time, have the power to make changes in your organization without being a part of your daily operations.

*...**pressing upon you*** is a host of uncontrollable forces you must work around. Ups and downs in the economy, industry shifts, vendor hassles, changing technology, environmental issues, and new competitive forces are just a few of the unknowns.

*...**standing directly in front of you*** is the enormous marketplace you must penetrate. The truth is, today the people inside this hallowed ground give little and demand much.

*...**and behind you*** is your organization, the people you hired to help pierce the marketplace in front of you. Do they drag you down, or do they propel you forward?

Make the effort to prevent 'I of the storm' pressures before they happen, instead of attacking them after they arrive.

The secret to easing these future pressures is realizing that the farther and faster you penetrate your market, the pressures from the top and from the bottom will fold back like the wings of an airplane. The deeper you penetrate, the less anyone wants to interfere with your momentum.

There are two things you can do now. First, understand that people are a common denominator in your pressures. One of your aims in hiring is to assemble a talent pool which shares your vision and values. Second, before you begin spending a lot of marketing dollars, identify why your early Start-Up Lane clients love you.

WILL YOU JUST TRY AND GRASP THESE TWO IDEAS AT THIS TIME?

This is I of Storm Napkinology one of three...next ABC...

Again, the challenge for you as a start-up leaving the lane is to try relieving the inevitable pressures before they arrive. And the answer is to penetrate the market as deep and as quickly as possible.

The deeper you penetrate the less anyone wants to interfere with your momentum, because everybody loves a winner.

The indispensable idea here is not better marketing, but assembling a talent pool that shares your vision and values. It is the people you hire that will help thrust you forward in the market.

People have personalities. Companies have personalities. Customers have personalities. The secret to your success and security is to align these personalities to create a winning match.

Managing your organization's culture is the silver bullet to creating an impossible-to-copy competitive advantage. It is your people who will provide the personal experience that solidifies your sales.

The reality is that each personality you hire, or each job responsibility you rearrange, will have an impact on the personality of your company. The success of your business is directly related to the interpersonal dynamics among your work force.

Who they are and how they relate to you and your employees shapes how they relate to your clients, which ultimately determines your future safety. Your hiring should not be left to chance – take it very seriously.

Pure and simple, mis-hires will hurt your company, other employees, and your clients. Unfortunately, start-ups rely a lot on 'blind date' 'gut instinct' hiring practices to build their team. They are gambling with their company's future more than they realize.

Start-up entrepreneurs should learn how to build a company culture that builds heart instead of heartache. This is not easy, but worth spending some effort to learn.

HOW GOOD ARE YOU AT PICKING THE RIGHT PEOPLE?

This is I of Storm Napkinology two of three…next ABC…

Again, the little known secret to reducing future 'i of the storm' pressures from top, bottom, front, and behind can be relieved if the business can just penetrate the market a deeper and a faster.

When everyone is making money, much of the noise subsides because again, having money solves a lot of problems that not having money creates.

Many owners who find themselves in the 'I of the storm' think about hiring a marketing consultant to help them. No time to learn and experiment. Hire outside brains. And, there are a huge supply of consultants out there willing to exchange their brain power for your money.

The majority of marketing pros will begin by dissecting the market. Demographers love this. First, they identify all the potentials to be persuaded and learn all about them. Then they test what messages through what media can give you the best possible chance for success.

WILL YOU THINK ABOUT THIS BEFORE YOU HIRE A MARKETING PRO?

Regardless of how bad of a business person you might be...you do have a few early clients right now that understand you and love you. As your business grows, you will gain some additional clients who will walk through fire for you. They will be loyal to the death, even if you are a bad business person doing bad business.

Before hiring outside marketing help, line up your loyal clients like they did during the Chicago St. Valentine's Day Massacre and ask them one question... "Why do you love me?" No, don't line them up...give them donuts! But still, ask.You may have to work a little on this...but there will be commonality in their answers. Yes, really. If you shape their common answer into your words and spread those words to as many people as you can afford...you will find that people who like those words will flock to you. Think about it!

This is I of Storm Napkinology three of three...done...

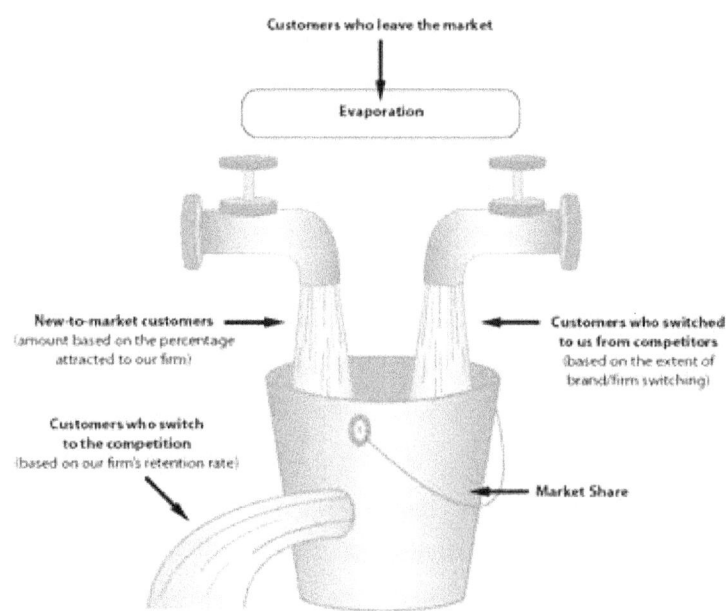

Customers who leave the market

Evaporation

New-to-market customers
(amount based on the percentage
attracted to our firm)

Customers who switched
to us from competitors
(based on the extent of
brand/firm switching)

Customers who switch
to the competition
(based on our firm's retention rate)

Market Share

Plug The Hole In Your Leaky Bucket.

This bucket is your business. Customers come to you from two sources, those who are new to the market and those who are not crazy about your competition.

Customers die or move, but most of your customers leave your bucket because they are not crazy about you. Your success is determined by the relationship of your faucets' intensity and the size of the hole in your bucket.

Your marketing regulates your faucet flow while your hole size is defined by your customers' experience.

Start-ups concentrate on flow. But, it's inevitable. Some tomorrow they will have to think about plugging the hole.

WILL YOU BE ABLE TO PLUG YOUR HOLE?

This is Leaky Bucket Napkinology one of one...done...

CAN YOU NOW DEMONSTRATE YOUR NAPKINOLOGY SKILLLS?

The Marketing/Sales Iceberg

Value Mathematical Formula

The 3-7-90 Rule

How Retail Traffic is   Increased

The Four Personalities

I of the Storm

Leaky Bucket

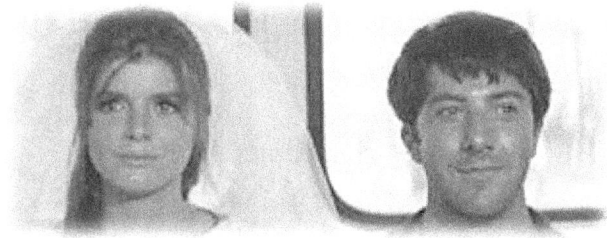

"Hello darkness, my old friend. I've come to talk with you again...."

There are many ways to demonstrate how important it is for you to understand value.

Simon and Garfunkle's lyrics to the 1967 movie *The Graduate* help demonstrate value. Allow me to reminisce about the movie.

From above the church altar Benjamin (Dustin Hoffman) bellows like a wounded animal down to Elaine (Katherine Ross), who is standing next to her pre-arranged groom. Elaine's soul suddenly catches fire and she screams out Benjamin's name. Elaine and Benjamin flee the church, fighting off their families with a crucifix, and then proceed to jump on a passing bus that will take them to their future.

The irony is deep. Benjamin was the newly educated individual whose tormented soul doesn't want to go into the corporate world of plastics. He does not feel connected to the circle that raised him. Instead, he searches for meaning. Elaine, Mrs. Robinson's daughter, who had not yet been graduated to the world of self-definition, is still passively controlled by her parents. Until their flight that is.

There is brief moment at the back of the bus when Elaine and Benjamin look away from each other with a wry smile on their faces. They are reveling in the fact that they have just ripped their lives away from every tradition they ever knew.

They have won the battle for self-authorship. What they will realize in just a few seconds is that they just forfeited their rights to inherited knowledge of the road ahead. Who will help them now? How would they find their way? Their world has suddenly shrunk to two people.

If you build your organization to help the Benjamins and Elaines...you will win their loyalty. There are a lot of Elaine and Benjamins out there struck with this enormity called life. They need help.

CAN YOU PROVIDE THE VALUE THEIR INTRICATE LIVES NEED?

"In restless dreams I walked alone..."

WHAT IS YOUR UNIQUE SELLING PROPOSITION (USP)?

Don't answer that because you probably don't have one.

The term USP was developed by advertising dude Rosser Reeves a long time ago. Rosser theorized that businesses differentiate themselves in the market place by finding and advertising a unique claim that the competition doesn't have. The claim, real or perceived, needs to be strong enough to have an impact the masses.

Forget USP and think *value proposition*.

A value proposition is a clear and concise statement about the results your potential clients will receive from your product or service. Its outcome is focused. It goes to the heart of the question of why your business should be patronized.

You want word-of-mouth talking on why you - not why you are different from others. This will help you identify the value you are offering. Then…. shout it to as many people your resources will allow.

Value Proposition Example…

The _____ Value Proposition of safety gives prospects and clients

a tangible, positive, bottom-line reason to select _____ over the

competition. Every Company interaction, both internal and external,

will reflect the Value Proposition of safety. _____ Safety Director,

Safety Account Managers, staff and employees will look out for the safety

of your company and your employees. Their OSHA and _____ field

safety training enables them to recognize and inform you of unsafe work

conditions and practices. _____ company-wide safety consciousness

will lower your company's risk for incidents and accidents. This will save

you money in the form of reduced insurance rates, less expensive medical care,

fewer repairs, less downtime, reduced investigation costs, and lessened fines.

In addition to generating more profit, your competitive advantage will

be enhanced.

"It was six men of Indostan who went to see the elephant (though all of them were blind)... that each by observation...might satisfy his mind."

-John Godfrey Saxe

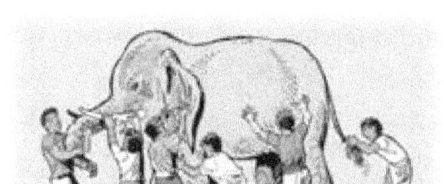

Each of the six blind men experienced the elephant in a different way. The first man felt the elephant's broad side and said the elephant was like a wall. The second man, feeling the elephant's tusk, thought the elephant was like a spear. To the third man, the elephant's trunk felt like a snake. The fourth man felt the elephant's knee and decided it was a trunk. The fifth man thought the ear was a fan, while the sixth man felt the tail and thought it was a rope.

Perceptual reality is subjective. It's the private, personal world people live in their minds, based on the truths they have accumulated over time. In terms of perceptual reality, each one of the six blind men was right in his perception of the elephant.

Many start-up entrepreneurs believe they have one group of people to influence – their potential clients. This is a huge mistake. There are at least five groups that you must recognize. These groups are your stakeholders. Stakeholders are the constituencies who have the power to accept or reject what you are offering. Your stakeholders are your partners, investors, clients, employees, and society. You may have more.

Each of your stakeholders has its own reality. They are the center and source of their own value. Turning these stakeholders into your supporters requires you to understand what they would value from their association with you. What a stakeholder wants is what they deem valuable. Your marketing efforts will identify what stakeholders want and deliver a series of experiences they will love. This is known as Stakeholder Relationship Management (SRM) and will be central to your success.

You want your stakeholders to be a community of people committed to a shared purpose – your purpose. Therefore, someone in your organization needs to be responsible for SRM.

WHO IS GOING TO BE RESPONSIBLE FOR SRM IN YOUR BUSINESS?

I just do not hear the concept LIFETIME VALUE used much in many businesses.

Sure, every once in a while I'll see some source give their interpretation of a customer's lifetime value to a retail store. It can't be correct for everyone, although I do applaud them for their effort.

WHY DON'T WE KNOW THE LIFETIME VALUE OF OUR CLIENTS?

The primary reason is that we don't seriously track the number of times our client has purchased from us over a specific period. We do seem to know our average ticket price but fail to multiply that times the amount of purchases in ten years.

The real number you are looking for is the potential value that your client represents as he walks through your door. Example: Average sale is $1,000. Average number of purchases over a ten year period is four (or three, or six). This client, over his lifetime of association with you, is worth between $3,000 and $6,000.

I guarantee your mindset will change if you know the lifetime value of your client and that every time he works with you are looking at a potential $6,000. And if you know his lifetime value, can't you better judge how much you are willing to pay to get him as a client?

It is feasible that you could lose money on the initial sale and still be profitable throughout the rest of the relationship. Video and book clubs figured this out long ago!

But, alas, many industries don't think like that. They must be profitable the first time because we may never see that client again.

His lifetime value is only as long as he is in front of us.

Or so it seems...

I fell in love with Sharon in the first grade. I blossomed early. The problem was that Sharon had no idea who I was, much less my infatuation for her.

What was a mature kid of six supposed to do? Well, I gave Sharon's brother Clyde my prized stack of alphabet cards in exchange for him telling his sister about the boy who worshiped her.

Little did I know that I had performed my first act of *advertising*. I had actually paid someone to tell my story.

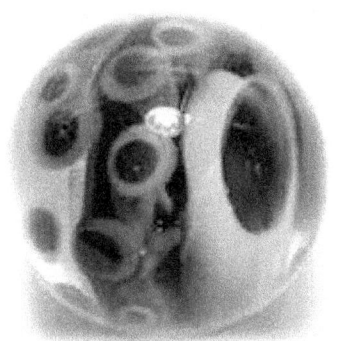

My shortcomings were that my one-time story stunk and Clyde, the paid messenger, didn't provide enough frequency to influence my target audience.

He really liked my prized bag of cat-eye marbles and he wanted to keep talking to his sister on my behalf in exchange for them. But I said no. I had to rethink my strategy and look for other ways to influence my would-be valentine.

I started paying attention to the way I dressed and the words I spoke. I made her laugh at recess. Later in life I learned that these clever methods I used to influence Sharon are what is known as *marketing*.

Simply stated, marketing is the multitude of tactics we use to get people to see something our way. It is everything we do and say to influence the thinking, decisions and behavior of other people in the world.

DO YOU THINK MARKETING AND ADVERTISING ARE INTERCHANGABLE WORDS?

Actually, they are not. Marketing is the alphabet, everything from A to Z. Advertising is just one letter. I did pay Clyde my marbles.

His advertising effectiveness did improve, especially when I surrendered a few baseball cards. I learned quickly that Clyde was just one part of my overall marketing plan to capture Sharon's heart. I wonder what ever happened to her?

Marketing is the big boy process of persuading people to do something in your favor. This is accomplished in two possible ways: What you do and what you say.

ARE YOU A TRANSACTIONAL BUYER OR A RELATIONSHIP BUYER?

My guess is that you are both.

Do you care where you buy your commodities? Toothpaste and milk are available on every corner. Chiropractors and accountants are numerous also, but you'll have to be much more selective about choosing their services because you will foster a relationship with them.

You got this transactional/relationship thing right? Transactional buyers buy on price. Relationship buyers buy on the relationship. Transactional sellers sell on price. Relationship sellers sell on...yep, you're there.

What you probably don't know is that only ten years ago, more of us wanted to buy based on relationships than on price. Out of ten buyers, six wanted to be sold on the business relationship and four just wanted the lowest price.

That statistic is pretty much reversed now. Six buy on price and four buy on relationship. Lots of reasons for that.

What's interesting is that, even ten years ago, sellers sold transactionally, not relationally. Today sellers still sell transactionally. They seem to have thought then and believe now that it's only about the price.

Price is important in the buying and selling equation but it is only a part of the personal experience received or given.

There's no harm in being a transactional or relationship buyer. But there is harm in not knowing if you are a transactional or relationship seller.

WHAT'S IN IT FOR ME?

Are you familiar with WIFM, the radio station most people listen to constantly?

WIFM is short for **W**hat's **I**n It **F**or **M**e, and it seems to be drowning out all other stations these days.

Have you noticed the slew of advertising for weight loss, curing baldness, and erectile dysfunction?

HOW MUCH ADVERTISING HAVE YOU SEEN RECENTLY THAT PLAYS TO POPLES' GREED, HUNGER, SEX, OR POPULARITY?

How much advertising out addresses peoples' overwhelming desire to be richer, happier, and healthier than everyone else?

Or how about parents wanting their children to be smarter and better looking? And...most of us want to stay young forever.

Today's most popular song is *Cheap, Fast, and Guaranteed*!

Yet, I constantly see advertising that doesn't even come close to mimicking these lyrics. The big secret is that you must play a song that gets on peoples' radio station, WIFM. You, your business, and your products must cater to the needs and desires of people.

The benefits of what your business offers must stimulate the growling lusts and needs of the emotional beast within people. You need a core marketing message that puts you head and shoulders above every other business.

And, you need a guarantee that helps eliminate risk.

Writing your version of this song is not easy. But, once written, your marketing record will get a lot more playing time.

Retail businesses love to play Transactional Poker.

Here's the deal. Consumers want to get the most and pay the least. Many retailers construe "most for least" as a price-driven directive. Their retail ad messages are straightforward sales, price-item, and event oriented – all intended to draw immediate traffic. This mode of advertising is commonly called *transactional advertising*.

Transactional advertising is intrusive, logical, urgent, and packed with an undeniable offer. However, it is commonly believed that effective transactional advertising can cause people to buy from you when, in fact, they really are not interested in what you have to sell. Wrong.

The truth is that transactional advertising interests only those who are in the market right now for what you have. And that number is only about 2-4% of your market at any one time. It's a small number.

To succeed in transactional advertising you have to sit down at the table with your competition and play Transactional Poker. In this game the player who intrudes the most with the best offer generally gets the bulk of the 2-4% traffic.

One hand per weekend, winner determined by close on Monday. A 'Half-Off Sale' trumps an 'Inventory Reduction Sale'. A 'This Weekend Only Sale' trumps a 'Coupon Sale'. A 'Going Out Of Business Sale' trumps all of them.

The result is like real poker hands, where you win some and you lose some. And if you sit one out you certainly lose. Hopefully, you'll win more than your original ante. If you don't, you might have to go home.

Transactional advertising messages can be carried by any media, including non-traditional media, but it is best conveyed through print. Many retailers learn quickly that the table stakes to play transactional poker are rising as the cost of media increases (and their effectiveness decreases). And, transactional advertising customarily generates lower closing percentages, lower average sales, and smaller margins.

YOU'RE NOT GOING TO PLAY TRANSACTIONAL POKER ARE YOU?

In every initial interview with a potential start-up, one or both of these questions arises: "Willie, would you like to take a look at some of my current marketing literature?"

…AND/OR …

"Willie, are you interested in examining the media I'm thinking about using?" My answer is "No, not now. I would rather go to the Dairy Queen."

What ensues is a blank stare accompanied by seconds of silence. "The Dairy Queen?" they ask. "Yes," I say. "The Dairy Queen. The place you start is your Market."

First, you must identify WHO it is you are attempting to influence, then WHAT to say to WHO, then HOW to deliver the WHAT to WHO. You must get the priorities right. It's Market, then Message, and then Media.

In many instances the start-up does not have a literature problem. The problem is rooted in the *identification* of the market. The days are long gone where you manufacture a widget and then try to figure out a way to sell it to the market. Marketing is a top to down process where first the market is identified, and then their needs are determined.

The Message and the Media become a lot easier when the Market is well identified.

IS YOUR MARKET IDENTIFIED?

Want to talk about it over a Blizzard?

"Not me! I'm innocent! I was framed!" This is the basic story of many incarcerated inmates in our criminal justice system today.

There are variations, of course, but "the establishment was out to get me" is the basic premise.

This was portrayed best in the movie *The Shawshank Redemption*.

Eddie Dufrane, played by Tim Robbins, was one of the new inmate fish being led into the prison, and the older "cons," led by Morgan Freeman, were gambling cigarettes as to what was his story.

In this movie Eddie Dufrane really is innocent, and he stuck to his story for about 20 years.

Eddie Dufrane's story was simple and he told it to anyone who would listen. He didn't develop it or change it while he was incarcerated. He told it from the day he entered Shawshank Prison until the day he left.

You also have a story. It explains the many reasons your potential clients should patronize your establishment. How you came to be who you are is what makes your unique creation story. Your story is also the value you have decided to create for your clients.

So I and the older cons are betting on your story.

"HEY, NEW FISH. WHAT'S YOUR STORY?"

Your parole board is located somewhere in your client's mind. He'll decide your fate - so your story (and value) needs to be impressive.

Edmund Hoyle set out to bring order to confusion.

His book of rules came to be accepted as the final authority to a 17th century card game.

When you believe you are proceeding "according to Hoyle" you believe you are doing things correctly.

Business owners who conduct their business "according to Hoyle" many times find themselves in difficulty. The reason is that many business owners live in a world of duality. Black-white, up-down, liberal-conservative, night-day, sale-no sale.

Year after year positions and business practices get entrenched, going unchallenged. They quietly sit, waiting for the world to visit their doorstep.

The fact is that what was "according to Hoyle" yesterday needs revised today.

The world is changing quickly. Why do we constantly compare numbers from the same month one year ago when the world and your clients are so much different?

AREN'T WE ANY MORE INTELIGENT, EXPERIENCED, AND SAVVIER THAN ANYTIME BEFORE?

Have we stopped learning?

Albert Einstein was giving his theoretical physics students a test when one student asked, "Sir, I think there's been a mistake. This is the same test we were given last year." Albert replied, "Yes, the test is the same, but this year the answers are different."

Your mission to create value for your client is the same as last year. Hopefully, your answers are different.

That's the way I see it, "according to Hoyle."

As he looked out over the perfectly manicured grass of the driving range at Augusta National, Sam Snead, in his mind was a kid again.

At 8:35 A.M. on Tuesday April 3, 2001, Sam Snead stepped onto the range to hit a few balls and to say a few 'Hellos'.

He ended up putting on a swing clinic. Very few golfers swing enough to make people stop and take notice.

Only one could do it at the age of 89 and that was Sam!

As Sam took his place and started to hit, one by one, Palmer, Watson, Faldo, and every other pro put their clubs down and gathered around, showing their respect and admiration for the greatest swing in golf history.

As ball after ball sailed into the sky, Sam raised his head and watched every ball find a home in that great green expanse of grass. He later admitted that at his age he couldn't see exactly where they landed. But he didn't need to.

"All I saw was green. But I could *feel* they were all good."

Someone else wrote the above story.

I share it with you to demonstrate the power of words and how a few letters can be strung together to paint a vivid picture in your mind.

Great marketing is not about being the slickest, cleverest, funniest, or most creative. Great marketing is your business's competitive advantage painted in your potential client's mind.

CAN YOU PAINT YOUR COMPETITIVE ADVANTAGES IN THEIR MIND?

What words do you feel will paint a masterpiece?

WHICH TWO PHILOSOPHERS BEST IDENTIFY THE REAL BATTLEGROUND IN WHICH YOU NOW COMPETE: PLATO, SOCRATES, ARISTOTLE, OBI-WAN KENOBI, or DEMOCRITUS?

The Force was with you if you selected Star Wars icon Obi-Wan Kenobi and Greek philosopher Democritus.

"Many of the truths we cling to depend greatly on our point of view," said Obi.

"Nothing exists except atoms and empty space; everything else is opinion," wrote Democritus (460-370 B.C). Wow!

Both of these quotes correctly identify the arena in which successful start-up entrepreneurs find victory – the target's mind! That's right! His mind. Many marketers incorrectly assume that they're fighting a product battle that is rooted in reality. They are preoccupied with getting all the facts right, analyzing the situation and making sure the truth is on their side.

However, the battle is not about having the best product. The battle is really for your target's perceptions.

Every day your target is bombarded by sights, sounds, smells, tastes, touches, and a gazillion advertising messages. He can't possibly process all the information that is upon him. He is not even asking for the advertising information. He selects information randomly, relying on his principles, experiences, interests, and needs.

Truth is not objective. It's subjective, depending on whose reality it is. What is true could be the same in your world but different in your target's world. Reality is then just a series of perceptions. A marketer's job is to introduce a series of mental images that positively shape your target's perception of your business. Yes, easier said than done. But at least we now know where the battle lies.

Democritus wrote that most everything is just opinion. I would hope that your target never hesitates to share his opinions. It gives us insight into his reality. Anyway, who is a higher authority than him? Certainly not you or I.

"Hello Darlin...Nice To See You."

These are the first six words of Conway Twitty's Greatest Hits album. A country classic. These six words illustrate one of the dirty little secrets in marketing. Everything begins in the mind.

People will only go to those places that they have already visited mentally. Your target will do nothing that he has not first seen himself do. His reality begins with his imagination. The objective of human persuasion is to cause your target to imagine doing what you want him to do. And, his imagination is an emotional right-brain function.

Scientific evidence has proven that music goes directly to the right-brain, bypassing the rational, analytical left-brain. The left-brain is needed to interpret the lyrics but it is the music that overrides the left and goes directly to the right-brain, evoking deeply felt emotional responses and pleasant memories. Again, to prove this you need only to hear one of your favorite songs and observe the emotion that it triggers within you. It is not a left-brain logical response. It is pure feelings.

Here are some selected lyrics from Conway's album that "talk" about visualization of the mind. Analyzing these lyrics from a left-brain perspective makes Conway look pretty selfish and petty. Put to music these songs and you'll understand how they have stirred the right brain of hundreds of thousands of music lovers.

"Now I'm lying here with Linda on my mind and next to me my soon to be the one I left behind."

"I've been to busy drinking, and she's been to busy thinking."

"She wore that falling out of love look. Still, the last lie I told her was the one she couldn't believe."

"We're not exactly strangers, you and I. I have already loved you in my mind."

Historically, most industries advertise and sell on logic when emotion is the primary motivator in most clients. Left brain calls unto left brain and right brain calls unto right brain. Successfully persuading your target starts with him seeing you in his world.

COULDN'T YOU USE MUSIC AND PRETTY PICTURES TO GET THERE?

"Goodbye Darlin...Gotta go now and try to find a way to lose these memories."

My wife and I found ourselves visiting Fort Worth's historical Stockyards. It didn't take much to conjure up images of cowboys, Indians, railroad workers, and buffalo hunters roaming the streets of one of the world's busiest livestock markets.

During the Wild West period thousands of cowboys had pushed millions of Texas Longhorns up the Chisolm Trail to Fort Worth to feed a growing and hungry nation.

On the open ranges of Texas, cattle mixed freely with animals of other owners. These unfenced ranges required cattle owners to practice the ancient art of branding. Branding simply identifies an animal by burning a distinctive mark on its hide. New owners burned a second brand and when a trail drive started a third brand help repel rustlers.

Wouldn't it be neat if a business was able to brand its loyal clients, establishing a special relationship that kept competitors away? Instead of the historical brand like the Four Sixes (6666) seen on a cow's rump we could burn in a business logo. Of course, this simply cannot be done.

However, burning a positive image about your business into your target's mind is certainly legal and good justification for spending marketing dollars. The objective of branding is to cause your business to be the one clients think of first and feel the best about when their moment of need arises. How to mentally brand your target varies from marketer to marketer. There are about as many theories as there are cattle brands.

DO YOU HAVE A BRANDING IRON?

Just an inside note: One of my classic western movies is John Wayne's Red River (1948). Two cowpokes who had been poking cattle for about a month are looking at one of their hand guns. Cowpoke A looks at Cowpoke B and says, *"There's only two things better than a good gun…a Swiss watch and a woman from anywhere."* It just made me laugh and has nothing to do with this ABC.

We think in pictures.

If you don't believe me, what image occurs in your mind when you look at the words....Washington Monument? What about...Golden Gate Bridge? You didn't scan each letter did you?

Let's try one that's not an object - a mother's love. What did you visualize?

We certainly want your target to visualize your business when he hears or reads your words. It would really be cool for him to visualize your business when he thinks about what you have to offer. In the world of marketing, this association is known as *branding*.

The big secret behind branding is *anchoring*. Anchoring involves associating the picture with a pleasant experience. When I say 'Disney World' or 'Las Vegas' the picture is much clearer if you have a positive experience there than had you never been there.

True branding occurs when a picture is associated with a memorable experience.

WHAT PICTURES EMERGE WITH THE WORDS *ROOT CANAL* AND *COLONOSCOPY*?

Your client couldn't possibly associate an experience with your business with one o these words could he?

PS: I know you have a story about the above cat. Your right brain is going nuts sorting out your cat stories.

Most of us are familiar with the experiment involving Russian physiologist Ivan Pavlov's dogs, the meat paste, and the bell.

Ring the bell every time you feed the dog the meat paste. Eventually, the dog starts to salivate when it hears the bell, anticipating the upcoming meat treat.

The Pavlov experiment proved the importance of associative memory to the branding process.

WHAT WOULD HAPPEN IF PAVLOV'S DOGS DIDN'T LIKE THE MEAT?

Well, the bell would have simply irritated the hell out of the dogs!

When your target hears your bell (or advertising), does he anticipate, salivate, regurgitate, or vacate?

My mother passed away over twenty years ago. We were close. One of the remaining items from her house was a simple wooden paper towel holder that sat on her kitchen counter.

I took that holder and put it in my kitchen, not thinking much about it at the time. Why? Well, I just didn't have one.

Little did I realize that this paper towel holder would be my best example of associative memory, the big secret to branding. In over twenty years I have not reached for a paper towel in my kitchen without thinking about my mother - all great thoughts by the way.

I think that if I replaced *that* particular holder with a new one, I probably would still think of Mom.

How easy is it for your client to associate positive or negative thoughts with your business after experiencing it? If he had a good or bad experience with your business, do you think it would be easy or hard for him to associate it with a particular object in his house?

This is why it's critical to create a great experience for him. He'll now associate it with the name of your business...MAYBE FOREVER!

WOULD YOU THINK OF MY MOM THE NEXT TIME YOU REACH FOR A PAPER TOWEL?

She was really cool! But then, you didn't have the opportunity to know her and associate her with anything but my testimonial...a little like advertising.

WHAT IS THE DIFFERENCE BETWEEN A LEAD AND AN INQUIRY?

Many large companies can't answer this question, and it has cost them sales opportunities.

You can keep your organization whole by understanding the following:

CRM: A CRM is a customer relationship management tool to manage and analyze client interactions and data through the client's sales process and lifecycle. You need a tracking system for this. There are multiple CRM systems available. 3x5 cards are the cheapest. Excel is efficient.

Inquiry: An inquiry is an interested party who has requested information and needs some level of assistance. An inquiry is not a lead.

Lead: A lead is a potential client that wants to learn more about what you have to offer. The client has acknowledged that they have a problem you could help solve.

A Qualified Lead: A lead that fits the profile of your perfect client.

Hot Lead: All about their degree of sales readiness.

Marketing Director: The person who is responsible for generating inquiries and giving the assistance needed to turn the inquiry into a lead.

Sales Associates: The people who take the lead from the Marketing Director and finalize the sale.

Customer Service Representative: The person who takes the sale to another level by embedding the product into the client's processes.

CEO: The person responsible for making sure all of these processes are well defined, that the proper individuals are assigned to these tasks, and that collaboration occurs between the two parties.

Lots of little links here that need to be connected, but you get the big picture.

And, of course, it is likely you are a one-person show now jumping on all the lily pads in your pond. If you start identifying the different roles you are playing now, your sales in the bigger pond will not be as complex.

Don't fall for ad agency nonsense about focus groups.

I've run enough of them to learn that they really don't work. Maybe fun to watch, but not relevant when you are trying to gather information that will keep you eating.

A focus group is a randomly selected set of people who are asked to give their opinion on new products or services before they are put on the market. For example, they might be asked to critique a new style entrée for a particular restaurant chain before it goes on the menu.

The reason they don't work is because people lie. Really. They want to please the questioner.

Want to learn?

1. Go to McDonald's and invest in some pop-psychology. Get yourself a Coke and sit near the large group of seniors that gather there each morning. Listen to what they are talking about. Before long you will be speaking their language.
2. Take your Coke and walk to the children's play area where all the moms are sitting and the kids are screaming as they run up and down the slides. It will take about 35 seconds to figure out who has control of their kids and who is about to shoot themselves.
3. As you drive out of the lot, think about how you would market to the people you just observed. At McDonald's, marketing is a course called How People Are Wired 101!
4. Take one of your early patrons who think the world of you to MacDonald's. Play 20 Questions with them while the moms and seniors live their daily lives. Don't stop asking and listening until you see the red in your client's eyes.
5. Start thinking about where you could go for breakfast in your town at 2:00 a.m. There is where you get your Masters in Pop-Psychology.

ARE YOU READY TO STREET LEARN?

Ancient Egyptian priests who prepared bodies for mummification knew a great deal about anatomy. This information got lost during the Dark Ages, and peasants very knew little about the heart.

Some believed the throbbing blood vessels in the legs and arms were a result of the heart wandering throughout the body. Thus people who were easily offended were said to wear their "heart on their sleeve." Those who were mortally afraid had their "heart in their mouth."

I look at a lot of jerks and con-artists among the players in business today. Sometimes, I think they're the majority. It's hard to do the right thing all the time, when it seems obvious that others are abundantly successful while doing the wrong thing. Their heart is buried beneath their bottom line.

My belief is that you can't fake value to people. Value must come from your heart, where you intentionally set out to offer a worthwhile product or service, and back it up with your generous and sincere expertise.

Loyal fans are created, word-of-mouth advertising begins, and sales go up. While this is not a guarantee that you will not have adversities, over time this action will have favorable results.

I often think we could earn a lot more baubles with some nasty "snake oil" selling tactics. However, your reputation is worth a lot more than money and I personally want my loyal fans watching my back.

I would rather be right than rich.

There are a many blessings in this life. One of them is to knowing a lot of people whose heart is in the right place.

IS YOUR HEART IN THE RIGHT PLACE?

If so, you'll have a lot of loyal friends.

CNA YUO RAED TIHS?

Olny 55 plepoe out of 100 can. Aoccdrnig to a rscheearch at Cmabrigde Uinervtisy, it dseno't mtaetr in waht oerdr the ltteres in a wrod are, the olny iproamtnt tihng is taht the frsit and lsat ltteer be in the rghit pclae. Tihs is bcuseae the huamn mnid deos not raed ervey lteter by istlef, but the wrod as a wlohe.

 Translation: "Can you read this? Only 55 people out of 100 can. According to a researcher at Cambridge University, it doesn't matter in what order the letters in a word are, the only important thing is that the first and last letter be in the right place. This is because the human mind does not read every letter by itself, but the word as a whole."

When people look into a mirror, what do they see first? They see the whole person.

So, like the words above, first and last impressions are important. However, your potential clients will judge their experience with you as a whole.

Do you tnihk lgrae eguonh wehn tnnkhig aubot tehm?

I don't understand political hit pieces where one politician attacks another because they changed their mind on something. Changing their principles…yes! Worth the attack. Changing their mind…no problem with me!

People make up their minds about things all the time. People can also change their minds. One of the primary goals of marketing is persuasion – persuading someone to do something that is in your favor. Most of the time that requires a change of mind.

The real question for a start-up entrepreneur to ask is…

WHY DO PEOPLE CHANGE THEIR MINDS?

The answer is that people don't change their minds. They just make different decisions based on new information.

Go ahead. Study your competition. Identify your product's features and benefits. List your competitive advantages. Identify your value proposition. But, you should think about how you are going to educate your potential clients about what you have.

Many believe that successful long-term marketing is educational-based marketing. I agree.

Educational marketing offers knowledge and enlightenment to your potential clients. It ignites their interest. If the information is useful it will trigger the sales cycle. It automatically positions you in their mind as an expert, ahead of your competition. You don't break rapport with an education-based approach. You build it.

Politicians who flip-flop weekly for support are foolish. Politicians who change their minds based on new information and can explain why will get my pass.

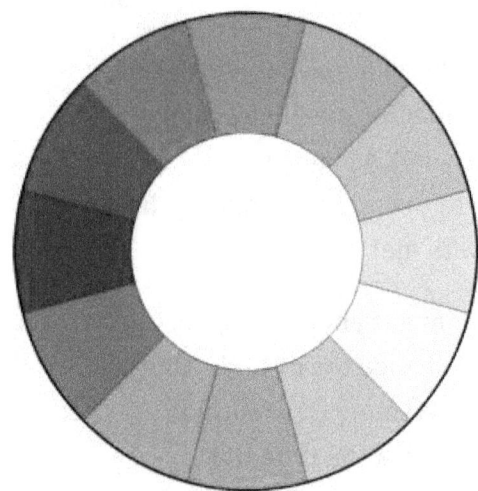

Two boxes.

Each weighs 25 pounds.

One is yellow. One is green.

Which is perceived as heavier?

The room is a pleasant 72 degrees. One week the room is painted blue.

The next week it is painted bright orange.

Which week is the room perceived as warmer?

Team A's dressing room is blue.

Team B's dressing room is red.

Which team is ready to tear you a new one and which team is ready for a nap?

By now you know that the perceived heavier box is the dark color, orange is perceived warmer than blue, and red is a fighting color. Color is a language and start-ups need to recognize this as they begin scaling up.

It is important to try to color match your product and service to the desired reaction you wish from your potential clients. Red side colors are warm and stimulating. Blue-Green side colors are cool and relaxing.

The affect colors have can come from many sources – everything from your logo to the carpet in your office. And for sure, don't let the geek who is developing the technical side of your website decide on colors without first talking to you.

WHAT COLOR IS YOUR LOGO?

Is there some thinking behind it?

Most marketing is neither awful nor great.

It's something more dangerous – ordinary.

We've all been taught to believe that average is the norm. Most people look like something between Quasimodo and Tom Cruise. Financially, most people exist somewhere between the homeless and Bill Gates. On an average plane trip you'll arrive at your destination. An average beer still tastes great on a hot day.

Average marketing that doesn't stand only accomplishes to spend your money. If your marketing is average, I recommend you keep your money! What you need when you leave Start-Up Lane is extraordinary marketing.

Most start-up entrepreneurs focus primarily on their products. The products have and continue to be the positioning difference. Basic product-centric marketing is very left brained. The appeal is logical.

If you put this approach into a dating scenario, it looks something like this…"Hey baby, I'm what you've been looking for since the first time you opened those big blue eyes." This is obnoxious, narcissistic, self-centered bragging. It's a quick hit, one-night stand approach to selling what you have.

The other side of advertising also goes back to Dating 101!

The hidden secret to extraordinary marketing is to communicate to others about things that are meaningful to them. Don't yak at them about your great product. Find an effective way to *win their heart*.

CAN YOU SHIFT YOUR THINKING TO SEDUCTION? Doesn't it make more sense to observe, study, and understand what 'turns them on'? And doesn't it make sense to communicate in a manner that is pleasing and meaningful to them?

The truth is there are probably as many ways to connect with people and seduce them as there are people to seduce.

The bottom line in Dating 101 is seduction through genuine emotional connection. Isn't what you want a trial (first date), repeat purchase (second date), brand loyalty (steady date), and a customer for life (really, really it)?

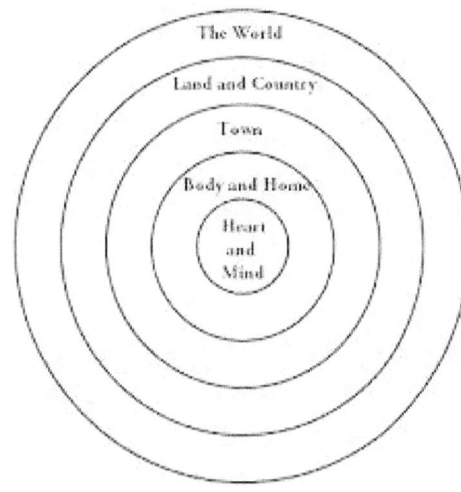

EVER HEAR OF ZENO?

Zeno was a Greek philosopher to whom the Stoic doctrine of *concentric circles of reducing empathy* can be traced.

In this doctrine, human caring radiates outward from oneself. Your caring diminishes as the distance grows, and increases as the proximity increases. Your empathy vanishes the further away you find yourself from the situation.

For example, the four hurricanes that hit Florida and the Tsunami in Asia years ago probably created no sleep deprivation for you, but you may have been up all night nursing your spouse's flu.

Everybody's problem is the biggest problem in the world to them – at that moment! Taking this idea to the extreme, you can reason that the destruction of the world is preferred to a cut on your finger.

Isolationists shout this doctrine while championing Fortress America. What happens in Syria does not concern us. Midwest lunch-bucket steel towns moan about job losses but think nothing about the Chinese lives greatly improved by the acquisition of those same jobs.

It's not that we are selfish or don't care. It's just that our lives are more complex than ever and we're just too darn busy living. In world of instant communication we seem to have more things to worry about, not less.

Understanding this doctrine of reducing empathy helps explain why people don't care much about your business, nor pay immediate attention to your marketing. It helps explain why your suppliers aren't as empathic to your needs as you wish. Or why your employees care less about your vision than a crisis at home.

Everyone has crosses to bear and nobody's life is perfect. Only when people are ready to purchase what you have is their innermost circle and yours much closer to being one.

Until then, you are farther away from her mind than Zeno himself.

This doesn't mean you roll over and die. You just have to keep working harder and smarter. Keeping this in perspective is really, really difficult sometimes.

CUSTOMER
SERVICE
DEPT.

www.guukaargen.com

"Who picked 'I Can't Get No Satisfaction'
to be our on-hold music?"

Don't sell. Serve.

Few people truly understand the power of great service. There is a passing parade of potential clients who crave what you have.

You have something of enormous value to offer them and you can prove it through your sales.

Be the big hearted lug that everyone turns to for help and you'll practically own peoples' pocketbook.

Service is a critical part of your value proposition. We generate leads, but it's your service and overall experience that drives client loyalty.

Unfortunately, people today feel that our service economy really stinks. As a nation we have become greatly dissatisfied with the service industry. It doesn't matter if we're talking about a trip to the doctor, a visit to the shopping mall, a phone call to the gas company, or a stop for fast food.

Whenever a service worker is involved, there are complaints. "No one cares anymore" is the bottom line complaint. The good quality service provided by the butcher, the baker, or the auto mechanic has become nearly extinct.

Dissatisfaction with the service industry in America has its roots in significant changes in the economic infrastructure that begin in the early 1900s.

Unsophisticated mom-and-pop retailers who historically thrived on excellent service are now being eaten up by those who provide a more convenient, technology driven experience...but one that is lacking in quality service.

The total package of a big box store has the initial attraction of what seems to be a better deal than the independents on Main Street.

Here's a question that should upset a few people.

IF IT'S NOT ABOUT SELLING, WHAT IS IT ABOUT?

The answer is service.

I am a frequent flyer member to multiple airlines. I am a Gold Member to a rental car company. I'm a Choice Privilege enrollee, Ready Card holder, Trip Rewards honoree at certain hotels.

Yes, I am a repeat customer - but I don't consider myself to be a loyal client!

A loyal client is someone who feels compelled to tell someone else why they are loyal. I can't remember the last time I was an evangelist for some company. Maybe I just don't believe that much in all the organizations that I depend on to help me make it through the day.

We clients rely heavily on family, friends, and colleagues for information about things we need or want. As our trust in media and advertising continues to wane, we cling to anything that helps us cut through all the duplicitous messages encouraging us to either buy or try.

Yes, we want to be influenced.

It's pure left brain then to believe that sales will grow in relation to how many people recommend us to others.

SHOULDN'T WE WORK HARD TO CREATE CLIENT EVANGELISTS?

Stop thinking big about your clients and "think small." Your marketing is not as effective when you tell everyone that your business is great. Your marketing works when you have one person believe that your business is great. You must think of your clients as people and not footprints.

Delta, American, Continental, Hertz, Holiday Inn, Comfort Inn, Red Roof, etc. treat me nice enough and reward me sufficiently to be a repeat client. That's just table stakes in today's marketing world. I'm waiting for someone to really knock my socks off and then I'll become their loyal advocate forever.

WHY HAVE SALESPEOPLE ALWAYS RECEIVED A BUM RAP?

Let's blame Arthur Miller. In the classic *Death of a Salesman* he portrayed Willie Lohman as a pathetic character who got by on connections, had little substance and questionable morals.

Let's blame Meredith Wilson who gave us the *Music Man*, a lovable rogue who would go to any extreme to con people into buying from him.

And how about P.T. Barnum's famous remark, 'There's a sucker born every minute.'? These are people who helped form the average American's view of salespeople.

Sales ranks among the least desirable of all professions. However, I'm here to tell you that selling is a tough job in which no one survives without competence, dedication, integrity, and a desire to succeed.

Salespeople live with their own initiative. They're constantly under the gun with generally more defeats than triumphs, more frustrations than fulfillment.

Both selling and leading a sales team are a process.

Your sales associates need constant attention, understanding, recognition, training, and perhaps most of all, leadership and direction. If you neglect them, their efforts will suffer and so will their morale.

Most salespeople welcome the coordination and direction of their efforts.

Without your leadership, Darwin's natural order of selection kicks in and only the strong survive.

That gives you a bum rap!

Answer this question:

DO YOU PERSONALLY GET EXCITED WHEN YOU HEAR THE WORD 'FREE' ANYMORE?

If you're like me you want to reject any offer that has this included in either the headline or the guts. The one word that used to rule the industry, now seemingly cannot even get on the key chain.

FREE is so overused that spam blockers bounce them off the floor of Delete Canyon. Ditto for the word NEW.

Here's another powerful word...RIGHT. How many times do you receive an e-mail offer so incredible that after you read the subject line you say to yourself, "Yeah, RIGHT", and then hit the delete key?

A mortgage rate of 1.95%! Yeah, RIGHT. Delete.

Beautiful women waiting for my call! Yeah, RIGHT. Delete.

Become a millionaire at home! Yeah, RIGHT. Delete.

Lose 30 lbs. in 7 minutes! Yeah, RIGHT. Delete.

When people sarcastically reply "RIGHT" to an offer, they think it's too outrageous to believe.

Yet we marketers work hard at developing hooks to pump up even bigger offers, having convinced ourselves that you can fool most of the people most of the time.

Well, I'm here to tell you that this is the road to WRONGSVILLE.

In today's world it's becoming more about stating a benefit and backing it up with strong, bold proof.

It's all about making an offer that doesn't trigger the response "Yeah...right."

Most discussions about the Three Stooges center on Curly and Shep. Who did you like more?

Moe, of course, was the ringleader.

Larry? Well, Larry was the most credible of the three-legged comedy stool. His quiet voice was one that brought some amount of sanity and believability to the crazy antics of the three.

In the marketing world, publicity's new nickname is Larry. Every start-up entrepreneur, including you, must be concerned with reputation. You have many stakeholders to influence (clients, employees, investors, creditors, govt. agencies, etc.).

Although many tactics and strategies can achieve good feelings about your competence and trustworthiness, you concentrate mostly on influencing your targets to pay attention to you.

Many start-ups begin by using paid advertising to spread their word. In other words, you pay some mass media to tell the industry your side of the story. Wouldn't it be clever to have other people talk kindly about you and your organization...and do it for FREE? Publicity is the general term reserved for getting positive press from the mass media WITHOUT charge.

Publicity can be a powerful tool in your efforts to influence your stakeholders. To generate this publicity you need to do something which is newsworthy. This can be something that a newspaper editor or broadcaster can ethically inform their audience. Good examples would be attending industry seminars or working with charitable organizations.

The discouraging part is that even though what you do is certainly newsworthy, your stakeholders are not interested in hearing YOU talk about them. They expect your story to be biased. They will, however, listen to others. They need a third party to bring some sanity to the clutter and confusion. They need Larry!

HOW CAN LARRY HELP YOU IN YOUR MARKETING EFFORTS?

Nyuk! Nyuk! Nyuk!

Our world is one of dueling concepts. Whatever exists has an opposite. Beautiful and ugly. Young and old. Rich and poor. Male and female. Let's continue. Up and down. Right and wrong. Left and right. Frequency and reach.

Frequency and reach? Yes.

WHY IS THIS DUALITY IMPORTANT TO YOU?

Because one of the mistakes that marketers make is too much reach and not enough frequency. Frequency is the media term for repetition. Reach is the number of people that hear your message.

In today's world your target is exposed to more marketing messages than ever. If marketing messages were rain he would be soaking wet. Unless your message has the same impact as that of the Kennedy assassination or 9-11, and it is very likely yours does not, then he will need to hear your message numerous times.

Many studies exist on the question of how many repetitions are necessary before a message sinks in. To summarize them, the simple answer is "a lot". Would you like to speak to 100 clients 10 times or 10 clients 100 times? Your best bet is the latter.

Many times we make a good offer but extend our reach too far, and with too little frequency.

In our world of dueling concepts, the best method is to shorten the reach and increase the frequency.

No-Man's Land. It was a piece of geography well known during World War I, Korea and Viet Nam.

It's the well defined area in the middle, directly ahead of two opposing forces. It is an area of peril and challenge.

You have a No-Man's Land in your business. It's only about three feet wide. It's the front door of your business. I would ask you to go there as soon as you finish reading this.

Face the world outside. Look at the cars speeding by, and the drivers and passengers currently oblivious to what your business offers. Look through the hills and city and imagine the hundreds of thousands of miles of Earth that are in front of you. Start counting the millions of people who don't even know you exist.

Don't count for too long. Ask yourself how many people in YOUR PRIMARY INDUSTRY don't know you exist.

Now, turn around. Look inside your organization. This is the area you can control – for example – the attitudes and abilities of your employees. The inside of your business and the outside of your business are two opposing forces.

You are standing in your No-Man's Land when at your front door.

Close your eyes.

DO YOU FEEL THE CHALLENGES THAT ARE IN FRONT OF YOU AND THE DIFFERENT ONES BEHIND YOU?

ARE YOU AWARE OF THE "BROKEN WINDOW" THEORY TO FIGHT CRIME?

Criminologists James Wilson and George Kelling formulated a premise that crime is the inevitable result of disorder. If a window is broken and left unrepaired, people walking by will conclude that no one cares and no one is in charge.

Soon, more windows will be broken, and the sense of anarchy will spread from the building to the street, sending a signal that anything goes.

Crime fighters in New York City applied this theory to the criminal epidemic ravaging the subway system in the 1980's. They believed that minor problems like graffiti on the subway cars, aggressive panhandling, and fare beating were invitations to more serious crimes.

It took almost six years to clean up the graffiti on the cars. A revamped Transit Authority cracked down on seemingly insignificant quality-of-life crimes such as littering, public urination, minor property damage, etc.

The results were dramatic. Tinkering with the environmental issues reversed the subway crime epidemic. Criminals are acutely sensitive to their environment and their behavior is a function of their social context.

Fixing the "Broken Windows" changed everything.

We certainly don't think your potential client is a criminal. Yet his purchasing behavior is affected by his surroundings in your business. He pays attention to the little things. Cracked walls, thin and worn carpet, paint chipped off walls.

You think it's about your products and your people. You might be surprised how much it has to do with the message you emit with your "Broken Windows."

Will you walk through your office(s) and inspect these aesthetic matters? It might help you create some value for your clients.

NYC subways graffiti is now art.

Many people assume that the quality of a decision is directly related to the time and effort that went into making it.

When doctors are faced with a difficult diagnosis, they order more tests. People uncertain about what they hear ask for a second opinion. Our children are told that haste makes waste, look before you leap, and to stop and think.

It seems like common sense to believe that we are always better off gathering as much information as possible and spending as much time as possible in deliberations.

However, research is telling us that decisions made very quickly can be every bit as good as decisions made cautiously and deliberately.

Go figure.

People start making snap decisions the moment they encounter your business. They will find the logic to support or deny their 'gut-driven' decisions. Their gut instincts will carry them all the way through your product delivery.

The more you understand what's important to people the better you are able to influence their snap judgments. It's not a perfect science, but understanding people may be what will get you in front of your competition – or behind them!

WHEN WAS THE LAST SNAP DECISION YOU MADE?

Zero ethics. That is what we have the moment we were born. By Kindergarten we were lying to our parents and teachers, and each other!

And here we are as adults, often still struggling to know what is right and how to do it.

Some years ago, a now former ad executive from a big agency known as Oglivy & Mather, was convicted of billing fraud and was ordered by the judge to submit a proposed code of ethics for the advertising industry.

In her 20-page report she states that a client's short-term financial pressures often put an agency's ethics at risk.

Should an agency do what the client wants or what the client needs? Is there a compromise? Is stretching the truth to the point that the marketing is misleading a breach of trust with the consumer or good business practice for the client (and the agency)?

Questionable ethics are not a competitive advantage in today's changing world. High standards will be a prerequisite for successful organizations of the future.

But you must remember that people's ethics vary as much as their personality. Doing the right thing is not always fixed or necessarily absolute. It's often ambiguous.

So, as the owner of your business you must set the standards. Violations of honesty and integrity dilute your ethical strength. Give yourself enough time to avoid ethical traps.

Reward people who tackle moral problems head on. Punish cover-ups. *And remember that anybody whose hands aren't clean can get the place dirty.*

Right and wrong are not black and white. Not everyone will be happy. But who said the journey is always easy and friendship is not all laughter?

CAN YOU WRITE A CODE OF ETHICS FOR YOUR BUSINESS?

To be a successful client-centric business you need to have the ability to seriously listen to your potential clients.

BUT HOW GOOD ARE YOU AND YOUR STAFF AT LISTENING?

Try this listening exercise:

Close your eyes and slowly count to 50 with one simple goal – don't let another thought enter your mind!

You must concentrate on maintaining your counting. My prediction is that you can't do it without distracting thoughts of anything other than counting interfering with this process.

The point is, if you can't listen to yourself, how do you expect to listen to your clients?

You goal is to allow your clients to feel special.

When you can successfully complete this exercise you will have a much greater chance of impressing them.

That's what you want, isn't it?

Everyone tells us that succeeding in business is pretty straightforward...

...focus on your clients and amaze them with experiences that exceed their expectations.

They will respond with repeat business and longer loyalty.

However, this simple, common-sense guideline appears to be more difficult than ever to accomplish.

Walls, T-shirts, and coffee mugs are depicted with statements such as ...

We are committed to our clients

or...

Our clients are the reason for our existence.

BUT HOW DO WE PUT THESE HIGH AND MIGHTY STATEMENTS INTO PRACTICE?

Let's start with you. Quietly answer these questions to yourself:

1) Are you passionately obsessed with making your clients happy every day, or are they the burden you bear because you weren't born rich or didn't win the lottery?
2) If you had all the money you needed and then some, would you still be energized every day by a mission to help others to solve their problems?

There's really no right or wrong answer here.

It's just a series of thought provoking questions to help you examine your level of commitment to a client-driven organization rather than a product-driven one.

DO YOU WANT TO COMMIT BUSINESS SUICIDE?

If they come to you because of your price, they will leave you for someone else's price.

If you want to have a short business life, play the low-price game. Here's the truth. There can be only one low price leader in a category. Second place dies.

And here's another truth. The low-price leader really does not have the lowest prices. They just have to be perceived as having the lowest prices.

K-Mart tried to fight the low-price game with Wal-Mart and lost. Target chose not to play this game. They became 'Wal-Mart'... with class.

Many small businesses tried unsuccessfully to play low-price when Wal-Mart came to town. They wound up playing 'outta here'.

Your marketing has two goals...attract new clients by promising superior value and keep them by delivering that value.

Don't play low-price unless you want to self-destruct.

Direct marketers call it 'selling the backside'. Major corporations refer to it as lifetime value. They lose money on the initial sale just for the opportunity to sell the backside. They know their numbers.

WHY DO WE THINK LITTLE ABOUT A CLIENT'S 'BACKSIDE'?

A lot of businesses focus on attracting new clients and recording the sales for that moment, week, or month and then comparing them to some sales numbers 900 transactions ago?

I'll venture a guess that you do not know the average amount of dollars your client will spend on your business over the next three to five years.

If I were to tell you that, on average, your potential client will likely give you $10,000 in business, would you be willing to sweeten the initial offer to get a shot at that $10,000?

Don't you think it would be smart to punch up some numbers on your computer and get an idea of their lifetime value to your business?

Forget lifetime. Just do five years.

I'm not asking you to lose money on the initial sale. However, I will guarantee you that once you know your potential client's lifetime value to your business, you will start to think about your initial offers a little differently.

Let's discuss the *rule of reciprocity*.

This rule says that we should try to repay, in kind, what another person has provided us.

We have all had situations in which people have done things for us and we are programmed to return the favor.

We feel obligated. Where do you think the phrase "Much obliged" came from?

Drilling into human programming has and is being utilized from fund raising organizations to the airport Hare Krishnas (remember the little flowers handed out before a request for donation?)

How do you think anything gets through Congress these days? It's just the rule of reciprocation on steroids.

People have been taught to live up to this overpowering rule. No one wants to be labeled a moocher, an ingrate, or a welsher. Studies have shown that people don't even have to like the person who extended the favor. They just need to get it repaid. Generally, a small favor can produce a sense of obligation that results in a larger favor in return.

For smart marketers this simply means that if we provide our potential clients a favor prior to a request, well, you get the picture. They'll have to do handstands to get that monkey off their back.

However, people are learning to say no to gifts and favors because they are now wise to the fact that it will cost them in the end. Yet, the power of reciprocity still remains. A favor is to be met with another favor. It is not to be met with neglect, and certainly not with attack.

So, our question of the day is...

HOW CAN YOU USE THE RULE OF RECIPROCITY TO BENEFIT YOUR BUSINESS?

WHO IS LES WUNDERMAN AND WHAT DOES HE HAVE TO DO WITH YOU?

Les Wunderman, a pioneer and advertising legend who is considered to be the father of direct marketing, believed that the client, not the product, must be the hero.

The product must create value for each of its clients. It must satisfy the unique differences among your clients, not their commonalties.

The call of the Industrial Revolution was manufacturers saying, "This is what I make. Don't you want it?" The call of the Information Age is consumers asking, "This is what I need. Won't you make it?"

When we develop our marketing we must think of clients in our market place as an audience of one. We must provide logical and emotional answers to the question of "Why should I buy from you?"

We should create a relationship that continues to grow, not just an isolated and one-time encounter. The better the buyer-seller relationship, the greater the profit.

That is why we need to create a marketing curriculum that teaches as it sells. Promotions may sell product trials, but they do not promote ongoing brand loyalty.

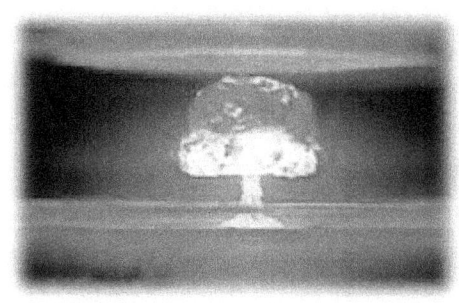

List all the great explorers who ventured into Earth's once-unknown regions.

Marco Polo. Columbus. Cortez. Magellan. Lewis and Clark...and countless others.

Now, add your name. Why? Because you are also an explorer of an unknown and dangerous region that no one has ever seen – the future!

It's a good thing our great explorers had not heard Doris Day's theme song *Que Sera Sera*: "Whatever will be will be. The future's not ours to see." Catchy, but wrong. We can never be sure of what will happen to us, but the great explorers of the past have shown us that the future is something we actively create, it does not happen to us.

As a business owner you need to think proactively, dream long term, and then seek out and actualize your chosen future. Imagine your business as one of the best in the country. Imagine hordes of clients extremely loyal to you. Imagine a staff that would walk through fire to work with you.

It was once said, "Almost anything can be done in twenty years." From the moment that President Franklin Roosevelt gave the order to build the first atomic bomb, it took only four years to do it.

When John F. Kennedy ordered NASA to put a man on the moon, it was done in only eight years. How long did it take Gates to build Microsoft?

DID ANY OF THESE PEOPLE FOLLOW DORIS DAY'S ADVICE?

Transforming your dream into reality can't be as difficult as developing the atomic bomb, putting a man on the moon, or transforming the information age, can it?

Believing that you have no control over your future and you should do whatever feels good at the moment is dangerous and foolish way to operate. You are a time traveler on a journey to the future. Explore your future possibilities.

Think Zebulon Pike or Ponce De Leon.

Not Doris Day.

Tennis is arguably one of the most strenuous tests of individual determination. No team here. One on one. Mono a mono.

A true tennis champion can withstand a 0-40 triple match point situation and battle back to victory. Why? Because it's one shot at a time – a 'do or die' situation.

You need to follow the lead of professional tennis players.

Clients today are not as loyal as they were in the past.

It's becoming foolish to believe that with all the choices and competitive parity that exist today people will stay loyal to your organization or brand for the rest of their natural lives.

Today they are loyal to your brand until you fool them, let them down, or another player offers them a better experience. Then all bets are off.

Your client's relationship is only as strong as their last interaction.

SHOULDN'T YOU START TREATING EVERY TOUCH POINT OF OUR ORGANIZATION AS A TENNIS DO-OR-DIE SITUATION?

Your website. Your initial phone conversations. Your physical presentation. Your delivery. Your follow-up...and on and on.

If you start thinking like the tennis player who believes that the only shot that counts is the one currently being played, then long term, Vegas odds will be in your favor.

Examine every touch point your clients experience as if you were down Love-40.

You might then avoid game, set, and match.

A young boy entered a drugstore phone booth and the pharmacist overheard the following conversation: "Hello, is this the Jones residence?...I would like to apply for the opening you have for a gardener...What's that, you already have a gardener?...Is he a good gardener?...Are you perfectly satisfied with all of his work?...Do you plan on keeping him?...I see...well, I'm glad you're getting such excellent service...bye."

As he left the booth the pharmacist remarked, "Johnny, I couldn't help overhearing your conversation, but aren't you the Jones' gardener?" To which Johnny replied, "That's right. I just called to find out how I'm doing."

At a very young age Johnny learned that the key to keeping his clients is to regularly evaluate what they like or dislike about his work.

WILL YOU CHECK UP ON WHAT YOUR CLIENTS LIKE AND DON'T LIKE?

Malcolm Gladwell, in his book *Blink*, makes a strong argument that our subconscious is what quietly regulates our world. In the depths of our subconscious, we make very quick judgments based on very little information. Our subconscious is our autopilot, thin slicing the world, and making decisions quickly and accurately, just as though we made them cautiously and deliberately.

This idea is the foundation of the one-question survey authored by Fred Reichheld. His book, *The Ultimate Question*, has gained the attention from many CEOs now for over 10 years. Reichheld accepts Malcolm Gladwell's premise that people know what they know but do not fully understand why they know it.

Your client's perception of you is your reality. Your desire is to measure their perception on how well you fulfilled your value promise to them. Reichheld's contention is that you would ask them one question and allow their instinct to answer it. One question - The Ultimate Question - and their answer will test your value proposition against their perception. Here's the question:

On a scale of 0-10, how likely would you recommend (**your business name)** to a friend or colleague?

This is NPS one of two...next...

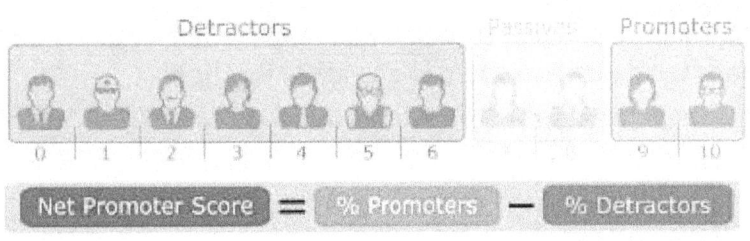

On a scale of 0-10 how likely would you recommend (<u>your business name</u>) to a friend or colleague?

Mr. Reichheld doesn't question your desire or initiative to satisfy your client. He questions how you know what your client is feeling and how you can be held accountable for their experience! He believes your clients are divided into three categories.

Promoters are loyal enthusiasts who keep buying from you and urge their friends to do the same.

Passives are satisfied but unenthusiastic customers who can easily be wooed by the competition.

Detractors are unhappy customers trapped in a bad relationship. They drive up service costs, demoralize frontline staff with complaints and demands. They grip to friends, relatives, colleagues, and anyone else who will listen.

Obviously, you want to increase the number of ***Promoters*** while decreasing the number of ***Detractors***. By answering this question intuitively your client will identify themselves a ***Promoter***, ***Passive***, or ***Detractor.***

By taking the percentage of ***Promoters*** and subtracting the percentage of ***Detractors*** your company can be assigned a ***Net Promoter Score (NPS).*** This one score becomes the basis for you to deliver profitable sustainable growth.

Example: 100 questions asked: 40% - 30% = 10% NPS

- 40 were identified as ***Promoters***
- 30 were identified as ***Passives***
- 30 were identified as ***Detractors***

WANT TO DIG DEEPER? Google Net Promoter Score. This is good client feedback in a nutshell.

This is NPS two of two...done...

In the 1700s European military leaders required their soldiers to march in tighter formations. A soldier's swinging arms must be able to touch his comrades on each side. If he could not, well, he was out-of-touch.

Many businesses are out-of-touch with their clients. We are convinced that if we provide a good service or product, our business will grow by word of mouth. In reality, people are too busy to market this way.

We think and market left brain messages of price and product, looking for a logical decision process. In reality, people are more emotional and unpredictable than ever. We work hard in eliminating people out of our selling process when in reality our clients do not mind working with people.

The difficulty we are experiencing traces back to our lack of understanding as to whether we are in a service industry or a products industry. Products are made and used. Services are delivered and experienced. Products are physical and impersonal. Services are personal and intangible.

ARE YOU IN A SERVICE INDUSTRY OR A PRODUCT INDUSTRY?

Personally, I think people are buying a service. People need to connect. They want to be associated with someone they can trust, someone who fits them like a comfortable pair of jeans.

As hard as we try, we cannot take people out of our business equation. But then again, my elbows are not in contact with anything, so I may be out-of-touch!

Exaggeration is built into the logic of marketing.

Space and time are limited and expensive. As a marketer you must select from many ideas and communicate only a few, maybe even just one, in order to gain a small foothold in your client's mind. Therefore it is important you "spin" that idea in the best possible light, preferably without misleading or creating misunderstanding in your market.

The idea you plant through your marketing only creates possibilities, they do not create realities. Your marketing makes a promise to your client about his upcoming experience with your business. If his experience contradicts your promise, well, you risk failure.

He is opting to make his views known within his network of family and friends, to his workplace, and to anyone who will take the time to research the Internet. This is communication you cannot control.

Recently a family I knew spent two days at the world famous Cedar Point amusement park. They chose to stay overnight, probably checking in at 10 PM and leaving by 8 AM. They booked rooms at a well-established hotel chain. One of them checked the Internet and found two comments posted somewhere that the bathrooms in this particular hotel needed some work. The family quickly cancelled the reservation and booked elsewhere.

Some stranger was dissatisfied enough to post information on a website and this family believed them. So much for the hotel chain spending millions of dollars a year promoting their values.

IS YOUR CLIENT TALKING ABOUT YOU IN THE SAME MANNER?

You better hope not! And you had better watch what you exaggerate. He's getting serious enough to fight back!

Clients do not know what items they routinely buy are supposed to cost.

Want proof?

Dig up some reruns of Bob Barker's long running The Price Is Right. This is the show where Bob tells audience participants to "come on down" so they can guess the correct prices of common, frequently purchased items.

Contestants are wrong about 50% of the time. This is real reality TV on which you should be paying attention.

If your client is not sure of common prices, why would you NOT believe he is clueless about occasional or unusual purchases like your product? In other words, he will judge whether your price is too high or not based solely on how you present it and will not be based on any of his own knowledge.

Of course, there are clients who research the price of major purchases via the Internet, consumer reports, or simple price shopping. This group is 10% or less and is mostly limited to cars, major appliances, swimming pools, etc. That leaves 90% who have only you to help them evaluate the value of a product or service.

The greater the value you create in his mind, the less price will matter. My guess is that you are selling everything for less than what you could. You might be selling less of it at lower prices than you would at higher prices. Think about that for a moment.

The lesson here is that price is NOT linked to your client's actual knowledge of what price should be or what comparable prices are. You have far more freedom and flexibility than you probably take advantage of to price as you please.

BY THE WAY, WHAT IS THE COST OF A TUBE OF CREST TOOTHPASTE?

"Catch and release" is a term used by fisherman who do not wish to keep the fish they caught. It's all about the *sport* of fishing.

Unfortunately, many businesses "catch and release" their clients. They dangle the bait (offers), hope the fish bite (leads), hook them (make the sale), and then let them go, only to move on to the next capture. And the next...and then the next...

They focus in on the fish they haven't yet caught.

This mindset is wrong, wrong, wrong! Sure, you need new clients, but you need to believe that when you "catch" your client you must work hard to keep him for life. No, you can't mount him on the wall. But you can do everything possible to build a healthy client relationship.

If you are good to your clients, they'll keep coming back because they like you. If they like you, they'll spend more money. It's a perpetual cycle that pays huge dividends – for everyone!

Your client, like the hooked fish, can sometimes enter into a buyer's remorse frame of mind. However, unlike the hooked fish, your client needs reassurance that he made the right decision and feels good about his experience with you. He needs to be reminded that you are always there for him, looking after his best interests, and not just for yours.

ARE YOU CATCHING AND RELEASING YOUR CLIENTS?

Or are you taking steps to build that long-term relationship?

When Wayne Gretzky was asked to analyze great hockey players he answered they always skate to where the puck will be, not where it is. Applying that insight to your business...

...DOESN'T IT MAKE SENSE TO SKATE TO WHERE THE MONEY WILL BE, NOT WHERE IT IS?

Businesses in your chosen industry have probably long believed that their competitive advantage and profits lie in their products. Yet, probably, there are multiple signs that the process of commoditization has entered their ice arena.

Commodity products are products perceived by your client to be readily available with little differentiation between them. Commodity businesses slug it out as margins shrink. You can think of them as skating to where the puck is.

The current reality is when your client becomes aware that he has a job to get done in his life, he looks around to hire someone or something to get that job done. Those skating to where the money will be are learning new things rather than clinging to past glory.

They are differentiating themselves away from their products and focusing on the jobs the client needs to get done.

Kid McCoy, now largely forgotten, was among the most colorful boxers of the 1890s. Outside the ring he didn't look very formidable.

People who saw him couldn't believe that he was the noted mauler. When his identity was challenged, Kid McCoy fired up and challengers found themselves face down in the barroom sawdust.

Kid McCoy had a reputation to live up to and so do you. Your business will have a reputation, good or bad. In marketing terms we call your reputation your brand, a term perceived by some as slick images that attempt to persuade your client that you are something which you are not.

Well, it is not you or your slickness, polish, or cleverness that makes your reputation your reputation or your brand your brand. It's whether or not you live out your promise to your client. It's all about the truth.

It's your responsibility to nurture, manage, and realize the extraordinary potential of your reputation or brand. Understand that you do not have a choice in branding. You are a brand. Understand that you should be true to your advertised message by living what is the essence of your brand every day.

Kid McCoy turned skeptics into believers.

ARE YOU THE REAL MCCOY?

Robert Preston will forever be remembered as "The Music Man." We've got trouble right here in River City which starts with a T that rhymes with P and that stands for POOL.

The River City juveniles who were playing eight ball could be straightened out by simply joining a band. Wow! What a concept. Identify the problem to a starving crowd and then offer a solution you just happen to have for sale.

Street-wise hustlers can take one glance at your eyes and know what you want. And, with a few coy phrases, they can give you the ammunition to convince yourself that what they have will feed your need. If they can actually deliver, you'll come back for more. If they're fibbing, they gotta leave town after the sale.

The first lesson here for marketers is very clear. When you're making an offer to your target be mindful that he can be swayed but, when betrayed, will quickly turn into a werewolf with teeth bared. What the large print giveth the small print should not taketh away.

These days, people are far more cautious and unwilling to be lead around by the nose. Unless you can leave town, I suggest your marketing be truthful, credible, and accountable. A pox on your house if you are not, as the universe deals harshly with liars.

The second lesson for marketers is that sometimes your potential client still believes you are trying to push 76 trombones down his throat. When this happens you must confront and smooth over his objections and complaints. He may not always be right, but he needs to know that he has been heard and that his complaints have been carefully addressed.

HOW DID PROFESSOR HAROLD HILL SOOTHE RIVER CITY PARENTS?

Well, he delivered a band good enough to satisfy the market. They were bad, but good enough for him to call River City home.

Horses were the method of transportation before the automobile. There were the splendid race horses that gave their all for short periods of time before being placed out to pasture. There were also the plug horses that slowly plodded along day after day, devoting their entire life to pulling carts and wagons. Plug horses long surpassed a racer's short productive life.

As you begin entering the marketplace it is appropriate to ask yourself...

"AM I A RACE HORSE OR A PLUG HORSE – OR BOTH?"

You sometimes perceive your plug horse business as a long and monotonous job, facing the same chores, with little end in sight. You also view your business as a race against previous sales numbers or goals, having just finished last year's sales race. You might even think you deserve a little pasture these next few months.

Well, sorry! Now is not the time to graze. Now is the time to plug along like a good plug horse should. Here are two questions you can nag yourself with as you take a bite of well-deserved feed.

Right now, what would really make my clients happy?

And, if I were a competitor of mine, what would I do to beat me?

Chew on those for a while...

Organizational narcissism can be broadly defined as an organization with an inward orientation rather than a customer focus.

 General Motors

Big business before World War I had a lot of organizational narcissism. You could start with Henry Ford. Remember that you could have any color of Henry's Model T as long as it was black? Nice client focus there.

In the 1920's organizational narcissism ran rampant, one of the biggest being General Motors. GM had a preoccupation with their products, production, and politics. GM knew exactly where to look to determine what cars people wanted – they looked in the mirror!

No one told them differently. That is, until Henry "Buck" Weaver!

Buck was an early pioneer in the field of market research and market-based decision making. In one of his published articles he wrote, "I am convinced that the approach of running a business from the customer viewpoint is perhaps bigger than any of us really realize."

Buck saw the consumer, including GM's customers, as the hub about which all activities revolve.

In the late 1920's and early 1930's, the GM hierarchy began to listen to Buck. And nothing happened. Sure, like a lot of organizations today, GM gave great lip service to the idea that the consumer was more important than GM the producer.

If customer loyalty was ever needed it was certainly during the Great Depression. Inside the inner circle GM assumed that consumer input was inherently undependable and thus could be ignored in favor of the well-entrenched inward focus on just producing automobiles. They just played the advertising shell game.

This contempt for people, against Buck's wishes, set the tone for GM and many of its wannabes until the early 80s. At that time the Japanese ate GM's lunch.

HOW DIFFERENT WOULD IT BE TODAY IF GENERAL MOTORS HAD LISTENED TO BUCK?

Your potential client's voice is important to what you do. Are you giving them a voice? And are you listening?

The first wave of baby boomers was born in 1946, which put the height of their childhood TV watching in the 1950s.

What early boomer didn't watch Superman defend truth, justice, and the American Way? What 65 year old can't remember Superman standing with arms folded as the beginning of the show while a third party testimonial told us how George Reeves, aka Superman, could move faster than a speeding bullet and leap tall buildings in a single bound?

It had to be the truth because he spent the next 22 minutes magically demonstrating it. Wow! What memories.

One of the single biggest marketing mistakes start-ups make today is not following Superman's lead and telling the truth! Many clients today have been conditioned to believe that selling is all about deception, whatever it takes to win the influence game.

The real secret is to simply tell the truth. We've talked about telling your target why he should patronize you instead of your competition. When you or your sales associate make a proposition, always tell the reasons why.

The more believable, embraceable, factual, and plausible your reasons are for patronizing your business, the more compelled he will be to do so.

A part of me still believes Superman is made of steel and his life folds like a cheap suit as the sight of kryptonite.

SO, WHY WOULDN'T YOUR CLIENT BELIEVE YOU?

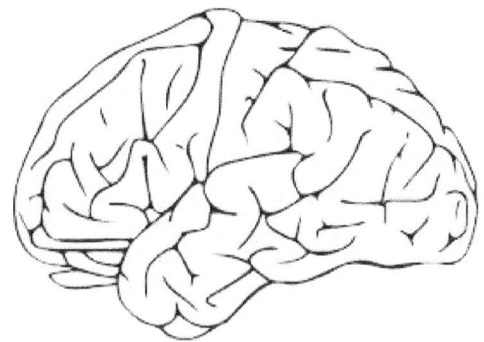

I don't' believe we were born with any ethics. The ethics we have were taught to us or learned from the school of hard knocks. Your business ethics will be the result of a lifelong process of development.

Unfortunately, many business owners easily cut corners, shave the truth, self-deal, and follow the crowd along the low road of least resistance. This is their standard of ethics.

People are looking for organizations that have a strong conscience. If you have questionable ethics and shabby standards you will find yourself crippled in the market place. If you demonstrate high standards you face a much brighter future.

It's hard to agree on what doing the right thing really is. You'll encounter circumstances that will leave you feeling there was no option but to settle for a compromised standard of what is right. Or, maybe your choice was to pick from a group of poor alternatives.

You're going to need a strong set of core values that will define your corporate nonnegotiable behavior and help you navigate through the gray areas. These core values set the parameters of rules and conduct for operating a business - the 'do's and the don'ts', the 'always, under any circumstances', and the 'never, under any circumstances'.

You core values should be clearly communicated to your employees so that they can be understood and followed. And most importantly, you and your leadership need to be true to those core values.

Excellent ethics don't come free. We all pick up some battle scars on the road to high standards.

HOW MUCH ETHICAL MUSCLE ARE YOU DEMONSTRATING?

"One thing. Just one thing. You stick to that one thing and everything else doesn't mean *%#."

So says the old-time cowboy in the film *City Slickers*. Well, I'm here to tell you again that the one thing for your business is the value you create for your clients.

Your clients and the value you create for them are all that matter to you. It's about them and their experiences, expectations, idiosyncrasies, preferences, personalities, energy levels, and their needs or wants...and how you satisfy them.

The value you bring to your clients lives solely in their heads. They will decide if you are valuable to them.

But, please know this...their decisions will not be made solely on your products' features and functionality.

Value has two other dimensions.

Economic value answers the question as to whether your product or service is worth their time and money. Psychological value is determined by the benefits that they are receiving are satisfying their emotional needs.

The simple fact is that if you can't find a way to meet your potential clients' needs they won't buy. Start by remembering to stick to one thing – the value you create!

SO, DOES YOUR MARKETING IDENTIFY WHAT THEY VALUE?

European noblemen as a whole were very vain. Ruffled sleeves, powdered wigs, black satin breeches, and full-length hose above buckled shoes were among the norm.

Many of the idle rich took pride in showing off a good pair of legs, some giving preference to one leg over another. To make a good impression, they learned to "put their best foot forward," a term we still use today.

Those in the 16th century knew something that we are relearning today. We crave beauty. We are born craving beauty. We stare at beautiful women. Tall, good-looking men are presumed to be wiser. Children paint with pretty colors. The truth is, we do judge books by their covers, cars by their image, and people by the way they dress.

We are reluctant to believe that our target has a subconscious conviction that the more beautiful choice is the better one. Many argue that it is substance, quality, and price that really count. Concentrate on the product or service, not any visual hocus-pocus.

Well, I'm here to tell you that you should always concentrate on your service or product. But also remember to do what the wealthy gentry did to attract many glances by putting your best foot forward.

Making your business environment more beautiful will improve your service and, subsequently, your client's overall experience.

WHICH OF YOUR LEGS ARE BETTER?

Let's face it. You want your client to be in awe after doing business with you. You really would like him to think "WOW!"

And you certainly want him to say "WOW!" to other people about you.

How is WOW achieved? Well, the devil is in the details.

(I like that line. It has been used forever to describe how one fails when implementing an idea, program, or just a simple task).

It is these same details that will "WOW!" your client.

No matter what you do or the service you provide, and no matter what presentation you make, the details you attend to are what convince your client that you care a great deal about him and are completely focused on his needs. Your client appreciates how you obsessed over all the little details that make his experience worthwhile.

At your first staff meeting have everyone make a quick list of things your organization could do to get the client to say 'WOW'.

WHAT ARE YOU GOING TO DO TO WOW YOUR CLIENT?

The legendary P.T. Barnum made his fortune on the insatiable curiosity and gulliability of the general public.

In one of Barnum's most outrageous "attractions" at his traveling circus, he advertised the opportunity to see "THE MAN EATING CHICKEN."

After paying to enter the tent, the circus goer found a man seated on a stool, happily gnawing on a drumstick.

I doubt if P.T. would be rolling over in his grave if he witnessed all the hype going on in this world. It appears that if you cannot make the ordinary extraordinary and the mundane fascinating then you can't make it in marketing these days.

Hype must be good because hype works.

I do believe in the sizzle. I also believe in the steak. If you have the sizzle and no steak you will soon be hoping people will pay to watch you eat chicken. If you have the steak and no sizzle...well, it may just be that all you need is some hype.

Do what you do so well – and so uniquely – that your clients cannot help but tell others about you. Now that's something to hype!

HAVE YOU EVER PAID TO SEE "THE MAN EATING CHICKEN?

I'll bet you have. If not Barnum's version, then certainly some other business whose sizzle promised much more than they could ever deliver.

Perry Mason never lost a case on TV. Never.

In just one hour, he presented his client's side of the story in a very compelling way, many times against all odds.

Imagine you are Perry Mason and you are standing in front of a jury box. You must make your case as to why your target should consider your business as opposed to all the other options he has.

You could just tell them they should believe you because you know what you are talking about. Or you could try to trick them with legal or marketing techniques.

Or you could bribe them with free gifts.

Personally, if my business life was on the line, I would be well prepared to give them all the reasons I could muster, and then proceed to support those reasons with witnesses, expert testimony, and even forensic evidence if possible. After my presentation, there would be no doubt in the jury's mind about choosing my business.

You don't have an hour to make your case, maybe only seconds.

ARE YOU PREPARED, OR WILL YOU LOSE PERRY'S FIRST CASE?

Learner and Lowe were pretty prolific songwriters.

From *My Fair Lady*, Freddie, the penniless aristocrat, sings, "I have often walked down this street before...but the pavement always stayed beneath my feet before."

These lyrics were in reference to his new love at first sight, Eliza Doolittle, who was inside dancing all night and concentrating about the rain in Spain. Yada yada yada...

Your potential clients may have reason to sing a similar song as they walk or drive past your business. Their lyrics might be, "I have often gone past your door before...but I never stopped because I have no reason to."

Learner and Lowe would have made it rhyme.

The most important marketing question you must answer is why *should* they stop?

WHY SHOULD YOUR POTENTIAL CLIENTS DO BUSINESS WITH YOU AS OPPOSED TO ALL THE OPTIONS THEY HAVE AVAILABLE?

If you answer this question successfully, you can start singing another Learner and Lowe *My Fair Lady* song, "I've Grown Accustomed to Their Face."

In 1257 King Henry III had a gold piece coined. His subjects didn't like it, much like we Americans didn't like our $2 bill. Not well suited for commerce but pleasing to the eye, the gold piece became obsolete and a valuable possession.

This spawned the term for any prized article being worth a pretty penny.

HAVE YOU NOTICED THAT YOUR CLIENTS SPEND A LOT OF PRETTY PENNIES?

Your client is proving over and over again how he is willing and eager to pay a premium price for a remarkable product. These products must possess higher levels of quality, engage an emotional response, and need to be at a fair price.

What's interesting about this is that s person will save and cut back across a broad spectrum of his budget in order to spend a disproportionate amount of money for an item or service that means a lot to him.

Have you ever asked yourself why Victoria's Secret, Starbucks, Panera Bread, BMW and a host of premium wines and lagers are attracting money in such scale?

Most people are too busy reducing costs and squeezing margins to notice that others will spend a pretty penny for one, two, or three categories that technically and emotionally fill their needs.

Hopefully your business is in the right place at the right time to be one of those categories. If we can just pause for a minute during our race to the price bottom we might learn that we could attract a lot of pretty pennies!

When Jimmy Johnson coached the Dallas Cowboys he was asked if he treated all players equally. He said, "If Emmit Smith falls asleep at a team meeting, we gently wake him when it is over."

"If the third string lineman dozes off, we trade him."

WHY IS THE WORD DISCRIMINATION PROFITABLE?

My current belief is that in marketing you *must* discriminate. While it may be philosophically admirable to treat all clients equally, it is economic suicide.

In managing clients, you must trim away the least profitable in order to invest more generously in those who are most profitable.

Will some of your clients will be more profitable than others? Should you consider pruning some of your least profitable clients from time to time? Should you invest more each year nurturing your Grade-A clients than your Grade-C clients? Yes, yes, and yes!

All customers are equal, but some are more equal than others!

The Ten Commandments Moses was carrying as he descended from the mountain had been carved in stone so that no word or letter could be altered.

Thomas Jefferson's epitaph has only 22 words carved into his gravestone. Unaltered since his death, these carved words refer to his authorship of American Independence and being the Father of the University of Virginia. His roles of Secretary of State and President of the United States were not mentioned. Jefferson was more proud of his efforts in independence and education than his national leadership.

Job descriptions are generally not carved in stone like the Ten Commandments or Old Thomas' gravestone. They are far from timeless and subject to change, many times on a whim.

However, a lesson can be learned from Moses and Jefferson. They aptly demonstrated that no job is ordinary. There are only people who insist on performing them in ordinary ways.

WILL YOUR PEOPLE HAVE ORDINARY JOBS?

You don't have to be Moses or Jefferson to understand that seemingly ordinary jobs can transform attitudes, experiences, and an entire culture, when they are done in extraordinary ways. Jobs are ordinary only if you want them to be.

Moses and Jefferson saw them as extraordinary.

So can you!

WHO IS IN CHARGE OF YOUR ORGANIZATION?

General Norman Schwartzkopf said, "When in command...take charge!"

Harland Cleveland says, "Nobody's completely in charge of anything."

I lean toward Cleveland's view when it comes to business.

In our high-tech age, if all information comes from the top, it's probably ineffective and too late. No grandpa at the helm possesses all the knowledge necessary to make an organization run efficiently.

Employees at all levels must be free to think for themselves – not just obey orders. As Cleveland says, "If nobody's in charge, the executive must minimize and define what everyone needs to agree on and maximize individual choice and ingenuity."

Your leadership is rooted in trusting your employees to do the right thing.

So let go of control and "turn 'em loose". If you've built a solid foundation, you'll soon discover that everyone is partially in control.

And I really believe this was true in General Schwartzkopf's military too.

Before the industrial revolution took hold cotton was spun in the household, very quietly. Progress and profits soared when mills replaced the individual weaver.

Machinery became a symbol of proficiency, and their distinctive sounds were linked with productivity.

When the machines broke down, the mills fell silent.

Dynamic and powerful organizations tend to keep moving. Organizations that rest will likely atrophy or die young. Many businesses are inclined to do nothing.

This looks good at first, if nothing bad happens. The downside is that doing nothing results in lack of motion. Active employees move on. Ideas become stagnant. When standing still becomes routine, eventually businesses go silent.

Stand outside a cotton-mill and hear the machines hum. Their movement creates progress. They go silent only for a short time because someone special is there to keep them humming.

CAN YOU MAKE THINGS HUM IN YOUR MILL?

Please, try to make your business hum. Doing nothing hurts you. Doing something will create progress, and inevitably, progress begets progress.

Right or wrong, keep moving!

In New York City I found myself standing on the corner of Broadway and 7th, waiting for the light to change so I could cross.

Standing beside me was a group of people with the same goal.

Directly across the street was another group of people waiting to cross to the exact spot on which I was standing. For a moment I visualized two street gangs who would fight their way to the other side.

When the light changed, about 100 people charged like the Light Brigade through the Valley of Death.

Surprise! Everyone got to the other side in about 15 seconds – without a scratch.

Everyone adjusted their approach to allow others to pass while still moving forward. The simple term for this is *mutual adjustment*.

IS MUTUAL ADJUSTMENT THE SILVER BULLET YOU"RE LOOKING FOR TO STRENGTHEN YOUR ORGANIZATION?

Well, no, not exactly. But, if you and your staff understand mutual adjustment, your organization will be much stronger. In a command-and-control organization the benevolent dictator-president would have taken hours to direct 100 people to cross the street.

In reality, 100 people left on their own, driven by a mission to cross the street, each adjusted their personal agenda to achieve the mission.

Today's world is one of creativity.

Humans are much more creative than for what we give them credit. Direct their mission and they will cross the street unscathed.

Try to micro-manage the whole process and you'll stop traffic for hours.

There has been a major shift in peoples' behavior that has changed the landscape.

People are better insulating themselves from the ever-increasing barrage of non-stop advertising.

Persuading people is not about bulk and muscle anymore because people are refusing to be pushed around.

Scarred experienced marketers know this and there is a sense of uneasiness about it.

We live in a world of that values and caters to instant gratification. Blue pills for erections. Yellow pills for more hair. Purple pills for whatever. Retail emergency liquidation sales for instant cash. Weirdo comedy.

Yet experience continually shows us the opposite. Abdominal surgery takes weeks to recover, weight loss takes longer than weight gain, and it takes longer to turn around an aircraft carrier than a sailboat.

Your marketing must be in sync, on target, and meaningful for people. Your marketing needs to reflect an understanding of the needs of your potential clients, as opposed to trying discover stronger persuasion techniques or elusive silver bullets.

To survive and thrive in these next years you will need to work hard to uncover the value equation lying dormant in each of your potential clients. You must find ways to make your businesses more valuable to your clients, and the answer is not just your products.

The secret lies in *serving* your clients, not *selling* to them. This is a significant shift in approach from time past.

CAN YOU THINK SERVE INSTEAD OF SELL?

It might save a life.

When man wanted to fly he first imitated birds by strapping on wings and jumping from tall buildings.

In your industry this would be called "best practices." It is the theory of seeing something successful from one business and implementing it into your business.

Many times the results are similar. No man successfully soared over tall buildings with strapped wings, so a best practice from one business is sometimes only marginally successful at another.

Changing your business for the better is about discovering the underlying causal reasons for your successes or failures. It's about identifying your circumstances and developing solutions that fit your situation. It's about understanding why something works or doesn't work. It's really not about copying someone else.

Don't take me wrong. I do not wish to dismiss viewing the best practices of others. What I am professing is that your business will improve with better thinking.

Someone finally thought thru the process and understood the relationship of speed and weight to lift under a wing. If you understand your problem you can reach a course of action based on your circumstances.

When your business is growing, you can manage it any way you want. Growth makes management easy. It's when growth stops that things get tough.

CAN YOU IMPROVE YOUR MANAGEMENT THROUGH BETTER THINKING?

IS "RIDING HERD" A LEGITIMATE MANAGEMENT STYLE?

In the days of fenceless ranching, cattle were driven to market by saddle driven leather-skinned cowboys "riding herd."

Cattle would sometimes balk, but generally they could be moved along without much fuss.

Many misguided business owners and sales managers expect to make ideas work by riding herd on their employees.

The truth is that humans, like cattle, love open ranges. They do not yearn to be managed. Talented and intelligent people despise the very idea.

When great companies are analyzed, "riding herd" on the employees is not cited as a positive technique. What gets noticed is the ability of the owners to create a business so successful that the employees stay and drive themselves.

It's the *purpose* that drives people, not a person.

Granted, you would go mad trying to lead a herd of cows by trying to give them purpose. However, people who are obsessed with a purpose need few directives, reminders, or motivational speeches. They organize around that purpose and work relentlessly to achieve it.

Don't ride herd on your employees. Give them a purpose for driving themselves and then get out of the way!

Here are some final tie-together thoughts.

Entrepreneurship is not about finding a clever way to sell a clever idea anymore. It's about sensing a problem, crafting a solution, and proving its value before offering it to the world.

Fire-in-their-belly entrepreneurs have a lot of help through their sense and prove stage. However, when their better mousetrap idea stands alone, they find no cheering parades and the help is now for hire. Becoming and staying the bright end of the flashlight requires increased marketing smarts once the idea is proven viable.

We've been moving out of the Industrial Age command-and-control organizational structure for a couple of decades now. If you are going to be an organization of the future you will build a community of people around a shared purpose.

Marketing is not a department. It's everything by everyone. Money will move to you because of value. Understand it mathematically (V=PE-P) and the vagueness goes away – so do business pressures.

Hone your creation story. Educational-based marketing beats advertising poker in the long run. Understand how mental pictures are created. Never forget that WFIM is everyone's favorite radio station…and more…and more…

There is so much more to learn…

You should have received a login to the website because of this purchase. I will be posting a new Marketing ABC each week for the next 52 weeks. You will be notified of each week's posting so that you may download.

Plus, the Beyond Start-Up Lane website will have a question and answer forum. You are invited to submit anonymous questions or comments through your login and I will answer as many as I can and post for all to see. It is there you can also identify marketing topics you would like addressed in future ABCs.

So, Beyond Start-Up Lane…   www.beyondstartuplane.com

WHATJA THINK? Go to the website and give me some thoughts….and keep moving to your rising

sun!

Willie

22 quotes to lift your spirits. These quotes were made by smart people who thought they could see in the future. After reading them, you should throw out any thought you have that on Start-Up Lane you are chasing a wild idea. The future is yours to control. Plus, here are some ads from the 20s and 30s.

"Computers in the future may weigh no more than 1.5 tons."
--*Popular Mechanics, forecasting the relentless march of science, 1949*

"I think there is a world market for maybe five computers."
--*Thomas Watson, chairman of IBM, 1943*

"I have traveled the length and breadth of this country and talked with the best people, and I can assure you that data processing is a fad that won't last out the year."
--*The editor in charge of business books for Prentice Hall, 1957*

"But what ... is it good for?"
--*Engineer at the Advanced Computing Systems Division of IBM, 1968, commenting on the microchip.*

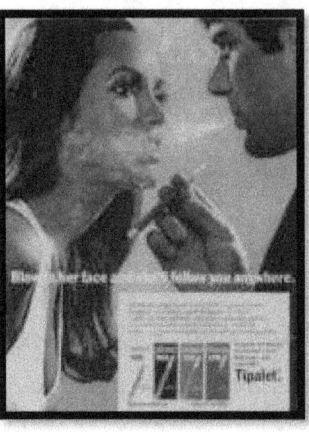

"There is no reason anyone would want a computer in their home."
--*Ken Olson, president, chairman and founder of Digital Equipment Corp., 1977*

"This 'telephone' has too many shortcomings to be seriously considered as a means of communication. The device is inherently of no value to us."
                            --*Western Union internal memo, 1876.*

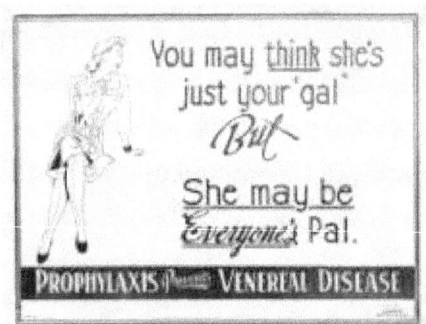

"The wireless music box has no imaginable commercial value. Who would pay for a message sent to nobody in particular?"
--*David Sarnoff's associates in response to his urgings for investment in the radio in the 1920s.*

"Who the hell wants to hear actors talk?"
--*H. M. Warner, Warner Brothers, 1927.*

"I'm just glad it'll be Clark Gable who's falling on his face and not Gary Cooper."
--*Gary Cooper on his decision not to take the leading role in "Gone With the Wind."*

"A cookie store is a bad idea. Besides, the market research reports say America likes crispy cookies, not soft and chewy cookies like you make."
--*Response to Debbi Fields' idea of starting Mrs. Fields' Cookies.*

"We don't like their sound, and guitar music is on the way out."
--*Decca Recording Co. rejecting the Beatles, 1962.*

"Heavier-than-air flying machines are impossible."
--*Lord Kelvin, president, Royal Society, 1895.*

"If I had thought about it, I wouldn't have done the experiment. The literature was full of examples that said you can't do this."
--*Spencer Silver on the work that led to the unique adhesives for 3-M "Post-It" Notepads.*

"So we went to Atari and said, 'Hey, we've got this amazing thing, even built with some of your parts, and what do you think about funding us? Or we'll give it to you. We just want to do it. Pay our salary, we'll come work for you.' And they said, 'No.' So then we went to Hewlett-Packard, and they said, 'Hey, we don't need you. You haven't got through college yet.'"
--*Apple Computer Inc. founder Steve Jobs on attempts to get Atari and H-P interested in his and Steve Wozniak's personal computer.*

"Professor Goddard does not know the relation between action and reaction and the need to have something better than a vacuum against which to react. He seems to lack the basic knowledge ladled out daily in high schools."
--*1921 New York Times editorial about Robert Goddard's revolutionary rocket work.*

"You want to have consistent and uniform muscle development across all of your muscles? It can't be done. It's just a fact of life. You just have to accept inconsistent muscle development as an unalterable condition of weight training."
--*Response to Arthur Jones, who solved the "unsolvable" problem by inventing Nautilus.*

"Drill for oil? You mean drill into the ground to try and find oil? You're crazy."
--*Drillers who Edwin L. Drake tried to enlist to his project to drill for oil in 1859.*

"Stocks have reached what looks like a permanently high plateau."
--*Irving Fisher, Professor of Economics, Yale University, 1929.*

"Aeroplanes are interesting toys but of no military value."
--*Marechal Ferdinand Foch, Professor of Strategy, Ecole Superieure de Guerre.*

"Everything that can be invented has been invented."
--*Charles H. Duell, Commissioner, U.S. Office of Patents, 1899.*

"Louis Pasteur's theory of germs is ridiculous fiction".
--*Pierre Pachet, Professor of Physiology at Toulouse, 1872*

"640K ought to be enough for anybody."